BREAKDOWN

BREAKDOWN

*The Pipeline Debate
and the Threat
to Canada's Future*

Dennis McConaghy

DUNDURN
TORONTO

Cover image: istock.com/mattjeacock
Printer: Webcom, a division of Marquis Book Printing Inc.

Library and Archives Canada Cataloguing in Publication

Title: Breakdown : the pipeline debate and the threat to Canada's future / Dennis McConaghy.
Names: McConaghy, Dennis, 1952- author.
Description: Includes bibliographical references and index.
Identifiers: Canadiana (print) 20190127007 | Canadiana (ebook) 20190127015 | ISBN
  9781459745087 (softcover) | ISBN 9781459745094 (PDF) | ISBN 9781459745100 (EPUB)
Subjects: LCSH: Energy development—Canada. | LCSH: Petroleum pipelines—Canada.
  | LCSH: Energy policy—Canada. | LCSH: Climatic changes—Government policy—Canada.
  | LCSH: Energy industries—Canada.
Classification: LCC HD9502.C32 M33 2019 | DDC 333.791/50971—dc23

1 2 3 4 5   23 22 21 20 19

We acknowledge the support of the Canada Council for the Arts and the Ontario Arts Council for our publishing program. We also acknowledge the financial support of the Government of Ontario, through the Ontario Book Publishing Tax Credit and Ontario Creates, and the Government of Canada.

Printed and bound in Canada.

VISIT US AT

 dundurn.com |  @dundurnpress | dundurnpress | dundurnpress

Dundurn
3 Church Street, Suite 500
Toronto, Ontario, Canada
M5E 1M2

For the children of Alberta — may you enjoy professional and personal fulfillment while preserving the ecological legacy of this province.

Contents

Maps

Foreword

CANADA IS FACING A CRISIS.

Hydrocarbon development in western Canada is stalled because of the seemingly endless delays in getting approval to build new pipelines and realizing their construction. Provincial governments and resource companies are united in opposing new federal legislation that will make it much more difficult to develop future major energy projects. Meanwhile, there is no national consensus on carbon pricing, which Conservative provincial governments across the country oppose. These circumstances are raising the spectre of a constitutional crisis.

Dennis McConaghy's *Breakdown* offers an insightful account of the challenges faced by Canada's energy sector in advancing and developing its natural resource bounty, and of the implications for all Canadians if those challenges are not overcome. McConaghy poses three crucial questions: Is it possible for Canada to have a national consensus that allows for the continued development of its world-class oil and natural gas resources? Do Canadians appreciate the value of these resources and their economic contribution? And, can hydrocarbon development be reconciled with a credible climate policy for Canada?

In trying to answer these questions, McConaghy explains the positions and actions of the competing interests involved in the debate surrounding hydrocarbon development. He outlines how the policy position of Prime Minister Stephen Harper clashed with that of U.S. President Barack Obama — particularly in the many frustrated attempts by Canada to obtain approval for the Keystone XL pipeline. He describes the tectonic shift that occurred in the Canadian political landscape in 2015 as a result of an NDP government being elected in Alberta, and the impact of the policies enacted by the federal Liberals after they returned to office that same year. The situation soon came to a head in 2017 with the frustrating intransigence of the minority NDP government elected in British Columbia, reliant on the Green Party to stay in power.

McConaghy is particularly critical of Prime Minister Justin Trudeau's attempts to reconcile the need for energy development with the creation of a credible climate policy, all while accommodating the interests of Indigenous groups. McConaghy argues that in Trudeau's attempts to please everyone, he pleases no one. Even the federal government's decision to buy the Trans Mountain pipeline from Kinder Morgan is greeted with skepticism.

Breakdown elaborates the quest for a grand bargain on the part of Alberta — a carbon tax and greenhouse gas emissions cap put in place by Alberta premier Rachel Notley in exchange for federal approval of much needed energy infrastructure projects. McConaghy rightly questions whether the efforts aimed at placating those opposed to energy development can ever be effective.

Breakdown comes at a time of great urgency for Canada. Profound decisions will determine many of the questions that McConaghy poses, and in so doing will determine what kind of country Canada is going to be.

As a journalist writing for the *Calgary Herald*, the *Globe and Mail*, and the CBC, **Deborah Yedlin** has been a pre-eminent commentator for the better part of twenty years on the nexus of business and politics in Canada.

Introduction

AT THE BEGINNING OF 2019, two impassioned Canadian protests took to the streets. For the United We Roll convoy, those streets began in Red Deer, Alberta, merged with the Trans-Canada Highway, and ended on Wellington Street in Ottawa, beneath Parliament Hill. Hundreds of workers arrived in their trucks to protest the threat to their livelihoods in the oil and gas industry — the threat caused by a decade of frustrated hydrocarbon infrastructure development and ineffectual political response.

Weeks earlier, other Canadians had demonstrated just as fervently; in that case, they were protesting against the construction of any such infrastructure. The RCMP had arrested fourteen people blocking the access of pipeline workers onto land in north-central British Columbia, access required to carry out pre-construction for a legally approved project. That pipeline, Coastal GasLink, would carry natural gas to Kitimat, B.C., where it would be converted to liquefied natural gas (LNG) and exported to Asia. The Canadian prime minister and the B.C. premier had endorsed the project heartily and publicly just a few months earlier. The protestors came out in solidarity with the specific subset of the local Indigenous community that had adamantly resisted this project for over four years, and with those who opposed any further hydrocarbon development in Canada on the grounds that such development increased the risk of global climate change.

United We Roll convoy protestors on Parliament Hill, February 2019.

LNG pipeline protestors, Vancouver, January 2019.

These protests exemplify Canada's political extremes — one imbued with a sense of absolute moral certitude regarding both its climate and Indigenous-rights demands, and the other "populist," not typified by dogmatic conservatism or corporate elitism, but rather motivated by the heartfelt reaction of workers trying to protect their livelihood. These respective protests perfectly demonstrate the division that has developed within Canada over the last ten years on the fundamental questions that are subject of this book: Should the country commit itself to hydrocarbon development as an indispensable contribution to its economy? Or should Canada eschew that opportunity as incompatible with contributing reasonably to containing the risk of global climate change? Just as significant in this discussion are issues of the appropriate limits of due process, what constitutes justifiable infringement of Indigenous rights, and to what degree these matters should be subordinated to the national economic interest.

Since the early 1950s, Alberta has thrived economically relative to much of the rest of Canada, overwhelmingly due to the development of its hydrocarbon resources. I must state at the outset that I spent roughly forty years professionally engaged in the development of hydrocarbon infrastructure and upgrading in Alberta, achieving considerable professional recognition and enjoying significant financial reward. In my experience, there was, prior to 2008, no substantive public policy debate that questioned such developments as inconsistent with the national interest or as representing some fundamental moral quandary.

Clearly, however, the recognition of the risk of global climate change caused by the rise in atmospheric concentrations of greenhouse gases, especially carbon dioxide (CO_2), beyond historic levels — attributable primarily to continuing human consumption of hydrocarbons — has put in question whether the world can continue to burn hydrocarbons such as oil and gas for fuel. The nature of the climate change risk requires global collective and coordinated action; in my view, catastrophic impacts are possible without appropriate mitigation and adaptation policy responses. But specific action to deal with the risk remains problematic, and global demand for hydrocarbons has not yet materially been reduced from historic levels. Indeed, that demand may in aggregate continue to grow for much of this century.

Reducing the risk of global climate change while sustaining levels of economic growth that rely on growing hydrocarbon consumption may prove an insuperable challenge globally, and the dilemma has become especially problematic for Canada. How will the country find an optimal mix of policy instruments to reasonably contribute to containing the risk?

Canada has participated in the UN process to deal with the climate change risk since that process's inception in the early 1990s. The country has dutifully imposed on itself national emissions reduction targets arising from various treaties and accords, from the one produced in Kyoto to the one developed in Paris, regardless of how much achieving such targets would cost Canada relative to the costs its major trading partners were prepared to impose on themselves. Canada has not yet achieved any of those targets. Since 1992 Canadian emissions have continued to grow. Unless Canada is prepared to impose massive intervention in its fundamental energy systems and contain or even contract its hydrocarbon production industries, it will come nowhere close to meeting its reduction targets arising from the 2015 Paris Climate Accord.

The threat, or moral imperative, of containing if not outright contracting the Canadian hydrocarbon industry lies at the core of those angry protests seen at the beginning of 2019. Indeed, it has had a material impact on the process of developing hydrocarbon pipeline infrastructure — over the past ten years, no new pipelines have been constructed.

How much is Canada prepared to go on sacrificing? How fair would that sacrifice be? To date, Canada has found no national consensus.

I retired in 2014 from my position as executive vice-president of one of Canada's pre-eminent hydrocarbon pipeline companies, TransCanada Pipelines. Since then, I have tried to be a constructive commentator on the subject of this fundamental challenge for Canada: Should hydrocarbon development be part of that future or not? As mentioned, I bring some forty years of experience both as energy executive and strategist; I believe that, as an engaged Canadian citizen, I can also contribute usefully to the debate.

In *Breakdown*, I argue that, despite the polarization that has emerged within the country, Canada can, and must, find a consensus that balances credible and proportionate climate policy — by which I mean policy instruments that contribute to reducing the risk of global climate change — with realizing the economic benefit of continued development of our hydrocarbon resources, specifically natural gas, primarily in Alberta and British Columbia, and the Alberta oil sands.

This book was completed in early 2019. The ultimate resolution of certain outstanding issues that are foreshadowed here, which may occur later than that, do not detract from the credibility of the analysis or the recommendations offered. They remain robust.

My first book, *Dysfunction: Canada After Keystone XL*, details KXL's journey from conception to rejection, and explores the consequences for Canada of the project's apparent demise. I was compelled to write *Dysfunction* because I wanted Canadians to understand how unfairly the country had been treated by both the Obama administration and the North American environmental movement. The failure to enact comprehensive carbon policy breakthroughs led to the nullifying of specific hydrocarbon infrastructure projects and the demonizing of specific resources, including the Canadian oil sands. Barack Obama ultimately rejected KXL to preserve his "climate credibility" before the late November 2015 UN climate meeting in Paris — his words. This rendered irrelevant the prior seven years of regulatory process for the approval of KXL, which had been substantively affirmative; multiple assessments conducted by the Obama administration's own Department of State had deemed KXL's incremental impact on global carbon emissions immaterial.[1]

Also distasteful and unfair for Canadians was the fact that, despite Obama's fundamental antipathy to hydrocarbons, his administration had abided a substantial increase in domestic crude oil and natural gas production over its tenure. Admittedly, breakthroughs in extraction technology had made that increase possible; still, Obama hypocritically allowed the United States to gain this economic benefit while unfairly depriving Canada of KXL. All of this took place even as Canadian carbon policy constraints became arguably more aggressive than what was unfolding in the United States over the same time frame — for example, this period saw the advent of carbon pricing in both Alberta and British Columbia.

I wanted Canadians to understand the costs Obama's decision had imposed on them, all in the name of "climate credibility." That lost additional pipeline capacity for future oil sands production meant that Canada would rely on more expensive rail transport in the interim, and over time that would result in lost production, costing billions of dollars in additional annual cash flow back to Canada.

Dysfunction was a book about how Canada was treated unfairly by elements within the United States. *Breakdown* is about what Canada has done to itself: about its failure to seize economic opportunity in its hydrocarbon potential, as evidenced by the building of no new pipelines, even while not developing a genuinely credible and proportionate contribution to dealing with the risk of global climate change.

But Canada — as the KXL experience reminds us so clearly — does not exist in a vacuum. American policy always provides a constraint on Canada's actions, limiting how the country may reasonably proceed, especially in respect of energy and carbon policy. The 2016 American election fundamentally changed the context for how such events in Canada would unfold.

Most Canadians, like most Americans, expected that Hillary Clinton would be elected president in 2016. I took no special pleasure in that prospect. In late 2010, in a moment of candour, then secretary of state Clinton had stated that she was inclined to approve Keystone XL, but that position was short-lived. She deferred to Obama after the project's denial became a litmus test for his "credibility" on climate change. Aligning with that position had, by then, become an absolute requirement of any politician wishing to remain a contender in the Democratic Party primaries, and Clinton subordinated whatever centrist impulses she may have had to that reality. As a presidential nominee in 2016, she duly announced that she opposed the KXL pipeline. Make no mistake: denying KXL meant denying incremental Canadian oil sands production, full stop. With Clinton as U.S. president, I anticipated greater negative consequences for Canadian hydrocarbon development, beyond continued resistance to KXL, than most Canadians seemed capable of acknowledging.

But, of course, the actual results of the 2016 election reversed those expectations. The message of an aging, crude, self-indulgent autocrat, moulded by the New York real estate industry and U.S. media celebrity, brimming with a lifetime of resentment and frustration with his country's evolution, had, incredibly, resonated with enough of the U.S. electorate to enable Donald Trump to be elected president. His election would give KXL a second chance, and would therefore allow for accelerated Canadian oil sands development. That was the new reality.

Trump's presidency would clearly be typified by an unshakable alignment with the interests of capital, seen as providing the only credible means for economic growth: lower taxes, fewer regulations, less redistribution of wealth. Regardless of what the Trump presidency would portend for America and the world, it was immediately evident that he was utterly indifferent to climate change risk and would fundamentally reverse how the United States approached the issue. The Trump administration would have no moral qualms about unfettering hydrocarbon production and consumption, since it was disinclined to consider climate change risk or other matters related to environmental sustainability as important. A Trump presidency would therefore provide a unique window of opportunity for the hydrocarbon industry, at least within the United States, to expand production and install infrastructure. There would be fewer federal regulatory constraints than could have possibly been imagined, given the evolution in regulatory oversight under the past administration. The energy policy of the United States would align fully with increased hydrocarbon production, and would be accompanied by a virtually nonexistent climate policy.

Would Canada seize these circumstances, recognizing them as opportunities to advance its economic interests? Canada did still have to question if Trump's impacts on carbon and energy policy would be sustainable. Did his presidency represent only a four-year hiatus from the international consensus to deal with the risk of climate change established at Paris in late 2015, or did Trump's election signal that there would be a genuine reset in how the world would deal with the climate risk?

• • • • •

On January 24, 2017, ironically the same day I launched *Dysfunction*, Trump announced that he would reverse Obama's decision and provide the necessary permit to cross the Canada-U.S. border that had so long eluded KXL. After another three months of process with the Department of State, Trump formally issued that permit to TransCanada CEO Russ Girling in person, in a brief Oval Office ceremony. Amity and alignment abounded; KXL was formally back under development. But as Girling observed to Trump as he accepted the permit, TransCanada still faced regulatory and legal challenges within the state of Nebraska. Nothing would come easy. The project's opponents would regroup and find new ways to obstruct KXL, resorting to the courts and state regulatory forums instead of the White House.

For Canadians, KXL's history should have led to one obvious question: Shouldn't we build the required infrastructure to realize market access for Canadian hydrocarbons, efficiently and responsibly, within our own jurisdiction, rather than rely on U.S. politics, regulatory structures, and judicial interventions? The building of various projects had been proposed within Canada over the ten years preceding Trump's decision, but to date, none have succeeded in being built. And so we must ask ourselves other, more fundamental questions: Can Canada find a national consensus to exploit its hydrocarbon potential and capture the attendant economic value? Do Canadians appreciate the scale of that economic contribution, and appreciate just what would be involved in replacing it? Or is Canada so fundamentally conflicted on carbon policy and hydrocarbon development that all it is able to achieve is protracted and unresolved approval processes that result in inevitable terminations?

Canada's political leadership has vacillated between support for hydrocarbon exploitation along with recognition of the country's economic dependence on hydrocarbons, and a fundamentally equivocal position typified by the aspirations of decarbonization and reinventing Canada around some ill-defined "green" economy. Although a modest majority of Canadians support hydrocarbon development,[2] Canada's basic political, regulatory, and judicial processes may be too broken to realize that potential, at least based on the record of the last ten years during which various projects have failed. So we have to ask ourselves: Will Canada permit economic contraction while the forces of obstruction and environmental extremism prevail in the long term? Is too much of the country simply indifferent to the consequences of losing the economic contribution of its hydrocarbon resources? Can Canada realize its hydrocarbon potential with a credible and proportionate national climate policy that is recognized as such internationally?

This book is not an academic treatise on Canadian energy and carbon policy, nor is it an investigative report into the confidential decision-making processes of the NDP government in Alberta and the Liberal government in Ottawa with respect to market access for hydrocarbons and carbon policy. Instead, this book is an essential history of how Alberta's legitimate demands for market access for its hydrocarbon resources have been frustrated over the last ten years. It also lays out the principles of fundamental policy change that would better enable Canada to capture economic value not only from hydrocarbons but also from all forms of major infrastructure development, while maintaining sufficient credibility in respect of carbon policy. Finally, *Breakdown* forthrightly confronts the choices available to Canadian political leadership on hydrocarbon development, and the consequences of those choices.

Part One of *Breakdown* discusses in detail events that occurred primarily within Canada from late 2015 to the end of 2018 — a period typified by continued frustration for those seeking market access for Alberta's hydrocarbons, incoherent national climate policy, and the continued failure of national institutions — political, judicial, and regulatory — to provide a functional approval process for major hydrocarbon infrastructure. It is important for Canadians to understand this history, not only in the context of hydrocarbons and climate change, but also in the broadest context of major development projects of all kinds. The question is whether the country retains the capacity to act in an economically rational manner, or whether the forces of obstruction have made a de facto breakthrough — a breakthrough to which too many Canadians may be entirely oblivious.

In Part Two, I suggest specific fundamental changes to Canadian regulatory processes as well as a national climate policy to redress the failures of the last ten years — years of lost opportunities. I propose fundamental clarifications of Canadian law that are inescapable if major developments are ever to occur with reasonable risk.

Canada may still realize the final available market access options, despite all the obstructions still in play. But we may lose those options. If we do, what fundamental political reaction will that evoke in Canada, and in Alberta especially? We will see more polarization and alienation, to be sure, but we may possibly see other, more extreme results — a breakdown not only of Alberta's economy but also a breakdown of the country — economically and politically.

PART ONE

The Problem

CHAPTER 1

Squaring the Circle

BEFORE DONALD TRUMP'S ELECTION to the American presidency in 2016, Canada had two remarkable election results of its own, one utterly astonishing, the other only modestly surprising. In May 2015 provincial NDP leader Rachel Notley became premier of Alberta, an entirely unprecedented achievement. Six months later, in October, the country elected federal Liberal leader Justin Trudeau prime minister of Canada. Each of these two leaders is the child of a political icon, an inheritor of a special political legacy that rejected right-of-centre priorities and empathies, and each was the beneficiary of a groundswell of support that spontaneously erupted in the course of their respective election campaigns. Trudeau championed a more diverse and tolerant Canada, one that recognized and strived to correct historic injustices while avoiding hard economic trade-offs through the magic of deficit financing. Notley wanted to guide Alberta to a more progressive political reality, less aligned with the corporatist priorities that had for so long dominated provincial politics. Similarly, she would rely on higher taxation and debt to avoid austerity. At the beginning of 2015, pollsters expected neither to win. But win they did.

Prior to her election in May 2015, Notley, despite her status as a major player in Alberta politics, was not deeply engaged in the conundrum of balancing Alberta's hydrocarbon potential with Canada's commitments to carbon emissions reduction as part of the United Nations climate process. Trudeau had espoused a kind of magical balance between the economy and the environment, relying on selective project approvals, a more sensitive regulatory process, and carbon pricing as a major policy instrument to achieve compliance with Canada's international emissions reduction commitments. Neither could have wished to be defined by this conundrum. But by late 2015 Canada was about to lose KXL, its most strategic market access option for diluted bitumen (also known as "dilbit") from the oil sands. Commodity prices for hydrocarbons had significantly declined from levels that once validated massive investment in the Canadian oil sands. American hydrocarbon production had grown, despite the Obama presidency, to the point where the United States was virtually self-sufficient in hydrocarbons for the first time in several decades. And the world was poised to embrace the aspirational goal of 2 degrees Celsius temperature containment at the Paris Climate Summit.

Trudeau and Notley would see much of their political record over the next four years defined by whether enough additional pipelines could be built to provide sufficient market access for Alberta's oil sands resource, and whether Alberta and Canada could simultaneously achieve sufficient credibility on the world stage in terms of how they contributed to dealing with the risk of global climate change. By the end of 2016 Notley and Trudeau would face the reality of Trump's presidency, a presidency characterized by an obsession with American self-interest, resulting in an animus towards the rest of the world, including long-standing allies such as Canada and the European Union, rationalized substantially by claiming that other countries have benefited from U.S. largesse, especially in respect of defence, while failing to provide it with sufficient compensation.

No one foresaw the possibility of a Notley majority government in Alberta until midway through the election campaign of April 2015. Her election was unimaginable until then, given the fact that previously there had been almost eighty years of conservative governments in Alberta. A unique confluence of factors led to her victory: vote splitting between the two right-wing parties, the collapse of the centrist Alberta Liberal Party, the unwillingness among middle- and lower-class Albertans to accept austerity as the policy response to lower commodity prices, accumulated resentments toward the ruling Conservative government, and fundamental changes in Alberta demography, especially in its two major cities, Calgary and Edmonton, where the populations were becoming more diverse and younger, and more receptive to progressive political alternatives.

As for Trudeau, six months before the federal election his Liberals lagged behind both the NDP and the Conservatives in popular vote projections, but admittedly not by an overwhelming margin. NDP support collapsed over the course of the fall election campaign as leader Thomas Mulcair moved to the right of Trudeau, espousing short-term fiscal responsibility over deficit spending. Trudeau also benefited from historic electoral advantages in Quebec and Atlantic Canada. Trudeau's majority win was surprising, but did not compare to the seismic shift in Alberta, where New Democrat support had increased from less than 10 percent to just over 40 percent of the popular vote since the last election in 2012.

Notley and Trudeau each replaced a long-tenured Conservative government committed to enabling increased hydrocarbon production. Federally, Stephen Harper had led a cautious right-of-centre government for almost a decade. Alberta had elected Progressive Conservative governments since the early 1970s. Both Notley and Trudeau offered more progressive, inclusive, sensitive governments that prioritized the interests of those segments of society historically marginalized. As distinct from Harper and the Alberta PCs, economic growth and competitiveness were not Notley's and Trudeau's pre-eminent priorities. Instead, these new leaders represented a more empathetic leadership; they would, they claimed, redress long-standing injustices and inequities, and they would preserve, if not expand, existing social welfare commitments, regardless of their efficacy.

As for who would pay, neither leader offered substantive answers. The answer, though, was intuitively obvious: all existing taxpayers would pay more through higher taxation, and, over time, via resort to increasing debt. Notley soon learned to recognize that she could not expand public services significantly, let alone sustain existing commitments, without an expanding hydrocarbon production sector. She had no other politically viable option to realize her policy ambitions. Ensuring improved market access for oil sands product became an inescapable imperative.

One must wonder if either Notley or Trudeau appreciated, at the time of their respective elections, how much their political legacies would be defined by how they dealt with the fundamental dilemma of rationalizing the country's hydrocarbon potential to credible carbon policy. In any case, that reality would soon become clear to them. Less clear was what their respective responses would be. To put it bluntly: it was not at all clear whether Canada would actually build oil sands pipelines or liquefied natural gas (LNG) infrastructure on the watch of these leaders. Would creating complex carbon policy prove an end in itself, regardless of its cost to Canada and especially to Alberta?

When Canada lost the KXL option in late 2015, both Notley and Trudeau appeared essentially indifferent. Neither expressed any real indignation about how Canada had been treated; instead, Trudeau pandered to the Obama administration. Notley was unable to acknowledge publicly the great value Alberta had lost by this denial. Other projects were in the process of being squandered, most notably Enbridge's Northern Gateway.

Prime Minister Justin Trudeau and Alberta premier Rachel Notley, Ottawa, November 2016.

At the Paris climate conference in December 2015, Canada again committed itself to a seemingly impossible-to-meet emissions reduction target — by 2030, the Liberals announced, Canada would cut its emissions by 30 percent from 2005 levels. However, the government offered no explanation for how such targets could coexist with increased hydrocarbon production enabled by additional pipeline capacity.[1] Neither leader would clarify the cost of compliance for these targets by Canadians relative to the analogous compliance costs incurred by Canada's major trading partners.

Nevertheless, in late 2015 Notley and Trudeau struck an implicit but essential bargain that tried to square the circle of climate credibility and growth in hydrocarbon production. Alberta would impose on itself a climate policy that the Trudeau government would accept as sufficiently credible, in return for an accommodation on Alberta's demands for market access for its growing oils sands production potential — albeit with the minimum necessary infrastructure. How this quid pro quo would jibe with the country's Paris climate commitments remained at best uncertain, but at least the country had almost fifteen years to figure it out. This chapter lays out how Notley and Trudeau struck their bargain, how it defined so much of the following three years of Canadian climate and energy policy, and its impact on the fate of the proposed infrastructure projects required for market access.

JUSTIN TRUDEAU ON CLIMATE AND PIPELINES UP TO DECEMBER 2015: "NOT HARPER"

Justin Trudeau was born in 1971, when his father, Pierre Elliott Trudeau, was prime minister of Canada. Unquestionably, Pierre Trudeau was one of the most influential and divisive of Canadian political leaders — a French Canadian who bluntly scolded Quebec that its identity was stronger within an officially bilingual Canada than as a separate country. He was willing to enforce Canadian unity even if that meant suspending civil liberties, which he did in 1970. He repatriated the Canadian constitution, imposing official bilingualism and a charter of rights and freedoms without any direct referendum on either, regardless of how profoundly they would change Canada.

For much of his tenure in office, Pierre Trudeau presided over a Canadian economy struggling with high inflation and inadequate economic growth (both of which he tried to solve through resort to wage and price controls); labour unrest, especially in the public sector; and the impact of two oil price shocks. After ruling Canada throughout the 1970s, Trudeau was defeated by Joe Clark's Progressive Conservatives in 1979. That government fell after a short time, however, and Trudeau returned to power early in 1980, continuing as PM until 1984. His traditional policy preferences would stand in contrast to those adopted in the early 1980s, most notably in the United States and United Kingdom, that led to the long period of global economic expansion typified by greater reliance on market forces, lower taxation, and monetary policy focused on containing inflation relative to other policy considerations.

Most notably, in the context of this book, Trudeau was the architect of the great bête noire of Alberta economic ambitions, the National Energy Program. Proclaimed in 1980, it was the culmination of his protracted interventions relating to the allocation of increased revenues from rising world crude oil prices between the federal government, Alberta, and the private sector. With grim determination, he asserted the primacy of federal power.

The government of Trudeau *père* would always be defined by its determination to promote national unity and its insistence on the paramountcy of the national interest. Ironically, these same issues now test his son. Almost fifty years later, those issues are still being discussed, but in the context of hydrocarbons, pipelines, and climate change. Vis-à-vis Alberta, Trudeau *père* dealt with how to distribute the wealth from hydrocarbon production, not whether hydrocarbon production and its resulting economic value should be realized in the first place. *Fils* deals with a more existential issue — can Canadian hydrocarbon production, let alone its growth, be justified in a world presumably seriously committed to dealing with the risk of global climate change?

Justin Trudeau, the eldest of Pierre's three sons, graduated with degrees from both McGill University, in his father's hometown of Montreal, and the University of British Columbia, in his mother's hometown of Vancouver, in literature and education, respectively. He formed strong personal connections to Ottawa, Montreal, lower Vancouver, and the north coast of British Columbia — areas that would come into play significantly in the context of the issues discussed in this book. Trudeau pursued a brief teaching career and followed that with a meandering pursuit of uncompleted degrees in environmental science and engineering over the early 2000s, as well as taking a leadership position with the non-profit youth volunteer service program Katimavik. In 2006 he began his political career in the Liberal Party of Canada — hardly a surprise. Significantly, he spent no part of his career in the private sector, and his income was essentially derived from a trust fund established by his father. In 2008 Trudeau was elected the Liberal MP for the east-end Montreal constituency of Papineau, and he was elected leader of the Liberal Party in the spring of 2013. Within three years he was prime minister.

Harper's Conservatives expected to convince Canadians that Trudeau was too callow and inexperienced, too insubstantial to serve as prime minister. That characterization made perfect sense given his resumé outside of politics, but ultimately, enough Canadians did not seem to care. Trudeau may not have been a typical Canadian with his unique privilege, lineage, and effortless bilingualism, but he was a near-perfect embodiment of the centre-left sensibility that a majority of Canadians have traditionally preferred politically. He would have no reservations over deficit spending or higher taxes. Moreover, he promised to reverse various Harper social policy priorities while supporting Indigenous reconciliation, gender equality, greater tolerance for all forms of diversity, and less alignment with American foreign policy.

This agenda, leaving aside the question of its economic sustainability, contrasted fundamentally with the priorities and basic affinities of Harper's Conservative governments. Trudeau was about as "un-Harper" as one could be, generationally, emotionally, and ideologically. He hoped to rally Canadians to their historic preference for progressive values, finding compromise between diverse national interests. But like all Liberal governments, he held out the implicit promise to ultimately accept economic reality and apply the appropriate policy when no other practical political alternative was available, just as Chrétien and Martin dealt with the Canadian deficit over the 1990s.

Notably, he had at this point no real connection to or affinity for Alberta. To his credit, however, Trudeau was forthright about his basic principles on energy, carbon, and the environment, even before his election as prime minister. He was committed to a position of balance. Of course, it remained to be seen how that would translate into specific policy and action. Essentially, he would not be Stephen Harper on climate change, environmental stewardship, or hydrocarbon boosterism, but he would strive not to alienate Alberta by explicitly rejecting growth in Canadian hydrocarbons. So, Trudeau's position on climate policy was a reaction to Harper's. The question was: What, substantially, was he reacting to — what was he so adamant to redress?

In the federal election campaign of 2006, fought between Harper and Paul Martin, climate change was not a prominent issue. Canada had, however, signed the Kyoto Protocol and committed to significant carbon emissions reductions, specifically a 6 percent total reduction by 2012 compared with 1990 levels, or roughly 460 megatonnes (MT). Canadian emissions had already grown by roughly 24 percent from the 1990 base year amount by the time of the election, and no one expected that a Harper government would impose carbon emissions reductions on the scale required to even approach Kyoto compliance. Harper held that meeting Canada's Kyoto commitments was simply "impossible."[2]

Still, that first Harper government accepted the political imperative for carbon policy, driven partly by its minority status in Parliament. In fact, Harper publicly acknowledged climate change as "perhaps the biggest threat to confront the future of humanity today," and "the defining issue for my generation." As a long-time critic of Canada's participation in Kyoto, he pledged an alternative "made-in-Canada solution." Harper's first effort was the Clean Air Act, Bill C-30, initially led by Environment Minister Rona Ambrose, an Alberta member of Parliament. The bill tried to shift the national focus to air pollution, not carbon emissions. It was introduced, debated, and significantly amended as the Clean Air and Climate Change Act, but never enacted. By early 2007, after intense negative reaction, Ambrose was replaced by Ontarian John Baird.

Soon after his appointment, Baird released the seminal discussion paper "Turning the Corner,"[3] which laid out how under Harper Canada would try to effect specific carbon emissions reductions, ultimately to be entrenched in new federal legislation. "Turning the Corner" detailed a regulatory framework based on improvements to various industrial sectors in carbon emission intensity — emissions per unit of output — not absolute emissions reductions. This formulation was compatible with an expanding Canadian hydrocarbon sector, especially considering that the technologies for extracting oil sands would likely improve over time. It included various compliance mechanisms in addition to physical emissions reductions, such as emissions trading options, lower non-Kyoto national emissions reduction targets, acquisition of domestic offsets, reliance on as yet unproven carbon-capture-and-sequestration technology and, to a limited extent, a $15 per tonne price on emitted carbon, which would go to a technology development fund. Aggregately, Baird's formulations ignored Canada's Kyoto Protocol commitment to reduce its annual emissions to 6 percent below 1990 levels by 2012, and created a new national target of 20 percent below the 2006 level (equivalent to 3 percent below the 1990 level) by 2020, or roughly 330 MT per year. For key industrial sectors, the cost of compliance remained ill defined, since it was difficult to predict the overall impact on competitiveness and availability of viable, affordable compliance options.

Consequently, the framework evoked no significant support from Canadian business. The Canadian environmental movement resented the framework as a major retrenchment from Kyoto, and remained unmoved by the Harper government's willingness to countenance elements of a national de facto cap-and-trade structure for, at least, large industrial emitters.[4]

But "Turning the Corner" established much of the basic modus operandi for Harper on Canadian climate policy: ambitious physical emissions reduction targets reasonably consistent with international expectations, but no resolve to impose specific regulations to achieve the targets, especially ones that constrained hydrocarbon growth. And it eschewed the policy alternative of a national carbon tax entirely.

The next federal election, in 2008, was the first with Justin Trudeau as a candidate. The Liberal leader, former environment minister Stéphane Dion, ran a campaign substantially predicated on his "Green Shift" concept — a national tax on carbon emissions, the proceeds from which would reduce other taxes or fund green technology. The election was in part a referendum on this explicit carbon policy proposal. The Conservatives castigated Dion's Green Shift as an unneeded and unproductive additional tax, despite its foundational tax revenue neutrality. The New Democratic Party did not support the Green Shift either, criticizing it as insufficient carbon policy and too lenient on large corporate emitters.

Dion's 2008 failure to make a compelling political case to Canadians for carbon pricing via a transparent carbon tax has had enduring political consequences, none of them positive. Harper was re-elected by dismissing out of hand a transparent, revenue-neutral carbon tax; however, he failed to form a majority government. What may have been good populist politics then has become a fundamental position for Canadian conservative parties since; as a result, they continue to suffer from a fundamental lack of credibility on climate policy.

All of this is rife with irony. Harper, widely acknowledged as the most conservative prime minister in Canadian history, eschewed carbon pricing via transparent, uniform, revenue-neutral carbon taxes, but for conservatives and the private sector such pricing was, and remains, the logical policy choice to deal with climate change risk, given that the alternative is almost certainly regulation. In early 2008 the non-partisan National Round Table on the Environment and the Economy federal advisory entity recommended a national carbon pricing policy for Canada to achieve "the greatest amount of carbon emissions reductions, at the least economic cost." Furthermore, the regulatory regime laid out in "Turning the Corner" would likely have cost much more than the Dion carbon tax, which was planned to begin at $10 per tonne and rise to $40 per tonne within four years.[5] But those points were lost in the excesses of political rhetoric during the 2008 campaign.

After the 2008 election, Albertan Jim Prentice was appointed federal environment minister. He had consistently been one of the more progressive and competent members of the Conservative caucus. Until the Copenhagen climate conference of late 2009, Canadian federal climate policy worked to perfect a national cap-and-trade scheme based on industrial emissions, aiming tangibly to improve on "business as usual."

But that policy initiative, not unlike "Turning the Corner," remained a perpetual work in progress. In fact, by the middle of 2009 Prentice had indefinitely deferred implementation of any actual regulations to effect national targets, ostensibly to enable more flexibility to ultimately integrate with a U.S. cap-and-trade regime — an outcome that never occurred due to the breakdown of carbon pricing in the Republican-controlled U.S. Senate in 2010 and beyond. At the Copenhagen climate conference, Canada committed itself to a new, voluntary emissions reduction target. The new goal was lower than what "Turning the Corner" had proposed, and more aligned with the Obama administration's target of a 17 percent reduction from 2005 levels by 2020, followed by 30 percent by 2030.

During Prentice's tenure, he collaborated with Alberta and its private electric generation sector, and struck agreements to phase coal out of the province's fuel mix for electric generation, potentially resulting in eventual emissions reductions on the order of 40 to 50 MT per year. However, that remained a one-off, singular achievement. Prentice did not manage to impose emissions regulations on the hydrocarbon production sector. Of course, physical emissions continued to grow within Canada, a function primarily of a growing national economy, which notably included a growing bitumen production sector.

Over the same period, 2006 to 2011, various provinces did take other climate initiatives. In 2007 Alberta started implementing intensity-based 12 percent emissions reduction requirements for large industrial emitters, with a compliance option of paying a de facto carbon price of $15 per tonne.[6] The proceeds of this tax were to advance carbon emissions reduction technology in the province, most notably through carbon-capture-and-sequestration pilots. In 2008 British Columbia's Liberal government established a revenue-neutral, economy-wide carbon tax, initially set at $10 per tonne and intended to reach $30 per tonne by 2012.[7] Concurrently, Quebec applied an updated hydrocarbon fuel-consumption tax, comparable in stringency to the emissions-based tax in British Columbia. Proceeds were intended to be applied to energy-efficiency programs within the province.[8] As well, Ontario was implementing a plan to phase out its coal-based electric generation capacity while initiating mandates for increased wind and solar capacity.[9]

In February 2011, just before the federal election campaign commenced, the Harper government announced that it would no longer pursue a cap-and-trade structure as the foundation of federal climate policy, let alone a transparent carbon tax. Instead, it aimed to introduce new mandatory rules and standards, mostly using existing statutory authority. That effort persisted right up to the 2015 election, resulting in no federal regulation on large industrial emitters or other forms of carbon emissions within Canada. In late December 2011, a few months after Harper realized his only majority mandate, Canada formally withdrew from the Kyoto Protocol, arguing that the cost of compliance for the country was untenable.

Shortly after Harper became prime minister in 2006, in his first major speech abroad he asserted that Canada was emerging as "a new energy superpower," and declared that his government would build Canada into a "global energy powerhouse." That statement defined his entire tenure as prime minister as significantly as all the Conservatives' ineffectual efforts on achieving credible climate policy defined it. How could Harper espouse such intentions and still commit to these various carbon reduction targets that would likely require, at least in physical terms, constraining hydrocarbon production growth in Canada? During Harper's tenure there was a massive buildup in oil sands production investment, a development that reflected the fact that the global hydrocarbon industry had come to view the resource as likely to offer sufficient returns to justify such investment. So, the resource would be a fundamental component of world heavy oil supply.

By the end of 2011 two oil sands market access projects, KXL and Northern Gateway, faced protracted regulatory approval processes, with resistance from the environmental non-governmental organization (ENGO) movement and great uncertainty over their eventual approval. The resistance was substantially animated by the incremental emissions impact attributed to the oil sands production enabled by these projects.[10] This should have compelled all Canadian politicians to confront seriously how Canada could rationalize the basic contradiction between Canada's hydrocarbon potential and its carbon policy credibility.

Trudeau, as a member of Parliament since 2008, had made no special contribution to the public debate on climate or energy policy. His position presumably aligned with that of Liberal opposition leader Michael Ignatieff, who disavowed the Dion Green Shift explicitly while urging the government to pursue aggressive long-term emissions reduction targets.[11]

Trudeau easily won the Liberal leadership in early 2013, with broad support from all segments of the party. His campaign for the leadership did not dwell on the specifics or nuances of carbon reduction targets, but he was clear in respect of specific oil sands–based pipeline projects — he opposed Enbridge's Northern Gateway on the basis that any risk of oil spills near the Great Bear Rainforest and the Douglas Channel was untenable. As I will explain in more detail later, he was at least conceptually open to the realization of TransCanada's Energy East, the KXL pipeline, and the expansion of the Trans Mountain pipeline (TMX).[12]

Later in 2013 Trudeau made a seminal speech at the Petroleum Club of Calgary, laying out his fundamental position of balance between credible carbon policy, including carbon pricing, and environmental stewardship. He accepted and welcomed the economic contribution from growing Canadian hydrocarbon production. Much of his speech comprised a critique of Harper for failing to deliver on KXL and on tangible carbon reductions while alienating too many Canadians with his hydrocarbon boosterism and climate skepticism. Trudeau's speech offered no specifics on carbon policy, regulatory reform, or new tactics for negotiating with the Obama administration on KXL, but he espoused a position entirely consistent with the inherent Canadian desire for centrist compromise. He took special glee in characterizing Harper as "a cheerleader, not a referee" for specific pipeline approvals, intimating that the Harper government's posture of advocacy for hydrocarbon development biased the regulatory system, tipping the scales unduly in industry's favour, to the exclusion of other legitimate considerations.

But Trudeau had no issues with the National Energy Board (NEB) approval of KXL. Furthermore, he attributed Obama's antipathy for KXL to Harper's lack of credibility on carbon policy: "If we had stronger environmental policy in this country — stronger oversight, tougher penalties, and yes, some sort of means to price carbon pollution — then I believe the Keystone XL pipeline would have been approved already." This critique had merit, although, in fairness, the Obama

25

administration had never proactively sought a compromise with the Harper government or conveyed publicly that appropriate Canadian carbon pricing might enable KXL's approval.

This speech, delivered in October 2013, again indicated that if Trudeau formed a government he would accept carbon pricing as a key component of Canadian carbon policy. His position evolved to having the federal government dictate the price's basic stringency and scope, while the provinces would implement those guidelines with their own chosen mechanisms. Of course, if provinces ignored the dictate, the federal government would act. This was a classically Liberal formulation that would have made Trudeau's father proud.

More problematic, however, was Trudeau's critique of the existing regulatory process for major pipeline infrastructure projects. That process, Trudeau claimed, was now tainted because the NEB had lost the "trust and confidence of Canadians." He stated: "You need a government, not a cheerleader…. The mistake this government made was in putting their thumb on the scale. The NEB is now, effectively, an advisory board to Cabinet. It is no longer a quasi-judicial body. So how can it grant the social license you need to proceed with big, complex, multi-year projects that require billions in capital expenditure?"[13]

This critique was never validated by any evidentiary process such as a government-sanctioned expert or peer review of the technical and procedural credibility of the recommendations proffered. Moreover, Trudeau never defined exactly what he meant by invoking social licence. The amorphous, problematic concept remained completely unreconciled to the actual regulatory approval processes. Was Trudeau implicitly promising those implacably opposed to hydrocarbon development that he would, if elected, change federal regulatory processes to ensure supra-regulatory consent?

Much of Trudeau's antipathy to existing regulatory processes was attributable to the NEB's 2013 approval of Enbridge's Northern Gateway project, a large-scale pipeline equivalent to KXL that would take oil sands bitumen from Edmonton to Kitimat, thereby providing tidewater access and market diversity. Trudeau and, even more importantly, his key political adviser at the time, Gerald Butts, had adamantly opposed Northern Gateway from the project's first public disclosure, regulatory process be damned. That regulatory process ran almost four years up to the NEB's recommendation of the pipeline as well as of the required tankers. The recommendation included over one hundred conditions on operations and construction, but it did culminate in an approval.

Trudeau and Butts had met at McGill University in the early 1990s, and they formed a long-term friendship that led to a political partnership as well. Butts was from a working-class Cape Breton family and was deeply aligned with the federal Liberal Party. After graduating in English and theology from McGill in the early 1990s, Butts worked in Ottawa for long-time Liberal Cape Breton senator Allan MacEachen. In the late 1990s Butts joined Dalton McGuinty in the latter's pursuit of the premiership of Ontario, and after McGuinty's election in 2003 Butts served as a key policy adviser responsible for Ontario's climate-related initiatives. His Green Plan restructured much of Ontario's electric generation infrastructure, imposing costs that would see Ontarians "choosing between paying the electricity bill and buying food or paying rent," as McGuinty's Liberal successor Kathleen Wynne conceded in 2017. Whoever said creating emissions reductions didn't cost?

In 2008 Butts took the helm of World Wildlife Fund (WWF) Canada, and he remained there for almost four years. As one of Canada's major environmental NGOs, WWF Canada adamantly opposed expanded hydrocarbon production along with all additional pipeline infrastructure that would enable such production, and it professed special animus for Northern Gateway.[14]

As CEO of WWF Canada, Butts made a speech in Calgary in early 2009. The contempt and condescension inherent in his words that day presumably captured his genuine convictions about the hydrocarbon industry, and, by extension, about Alberta: "You guys have gotten everything you've ever wanted, and you're going to find it's way more difficult to get things done."[15] This amounted to a direct threat; the creation of energy infrastructure would soon be made very difficult as a result of greater obstruction. Did Butts believe that dealing with climate change would require sacrificing the Canadian hydrocarbon industry? What else could he have meant? This certainly seemed to be his mindset circa 2012.

Not surprisingly, once Trudeau announced his intention to seek the Liberal leadership in 2012, Butts left WWF to join Trudeau as his closest policy adviser and political strategist. Soon after, Trudeau declared his absolute opposition to Northern Gateway, citing that any spill risk in the area proximate to Kitimat was intolerable.

Going into 2015 Trudeau maintained a position distinct from the Conservatives: he insisted that carbon pricing was an essential component of Canadian carbon policy while at the same time offering the Alberta energy sector selective pipeline support. This was a potentially reasonable consensus position, provided one could ignore his dubious musings on regulatory reform, his irrational opposition to the Northern Gateway regulatory process, and his principal policy adviser's historical antipathy to any further hydrocarbon expansion in Canada. The Mulcair NDP had never found a major oil sands based pipeline project it could abide, supporting only ever more extreme emissions reduction targets. And the Harper Conservatives remained adamantly opposed to any transparent carbon pricing via carbon taxes.

In early 2015, just a few months before the formal election campaign commenced, Trudeau delivered another speech at the Petroleum Club, again extolling balance between the economic value offered by hydrocarbons and environmental policy. This time he clarified that national emissions reduction targets and carbon pricing standards would be set federally, while, ideally, the provinces would implement their own strategies. He clearly believed significant national carbon emissions reductions could coexist with expanding hydrocarbon production, but he did not acknowledge just how difficult meeting such targets must prove, especially for a country that had already substantially decarbonized its electric generation sector, and that had a significant heavy oil and natural gas endowment. Up to his election, Trudeau never offered a fact-based explanation of how emissions reduction targets could be met while at the same time oil sands and LNG production was expanding. He did, however, promise to genuinely try to square that circle, without the cynicism and disingenuousness he ascribed to Harper. For the purposes of his 2015 election campaign, that was enough.

It is important to understand some basic numbers of Canadian "carbon math," as they stood at that point. In the spring of 2015, the Harper government had submitted to the United Nations Canada's emissions reduction targets for the Paris Climate Accord: dropping to 17 percent below 2005 levels by 2020, and to 30 percent by 2030 — roughly 250 MT annually. Harper essentially reapplied Canada's voluntary reduction commitment from the Copenhagen climate conference. If Canada increased its oil sands production during that same period by 1 to 1.5 million barrels per day, Canadian carbon emissions would not decrease; in fact, they would increase by 30 to 50 MT annually, barring some unpredictable technology breakthrough in basic in situ recovery technology.[16]

Prospective LNG exports also stood to materially increase Canadian emissions; each world-scale project could add close to 10 MT annually.[17] Any growth in the Canadian economy would also increase emissions modestly, unless massive interventions forced Canadians to consume less energy. At best, closing Alberta coal-based generation by 2030 would provide 30 to 40 MT of annual reductions.

The math is clear. What was not at all clear was what level of pricing or intervention would be countenanced to meet these targets. Trudeau never publicly acknowledged either the stark reality revealed by the carbon math or the specifics of the policy that would deal with it — any more than Harper had. Canada has very few "cheap" emissions-reduction alternatives, certainly compared with the United States. Conforming to American emissions reduction targets would cost Canada relatively and substantially more. And — of course — those targets were affirmed in December 2015, as Canada participated in the Paris Climate Accord commitment.

Trudeau happily asserted in Paris that "Canada can view climate change not just as a challenge but as an historic opportunity. An opportunity to build a sustainable economy, based on clean technology, on green infrastructure, and on green jobs." He told the world: "We will not sacrifice growth; we will create growth. We will do more to address the global challenge of climate change."[18]

RACHEL NOTLEY AND ALBERTA'S PROGRESSIVE CLIMATE POLICY

Six months before Trudeau became prime minister, in May 2015 Alberta elected its first centre-left government in roughly eighty years. Rachel Notley's New Democrats gained roughly 40 percent of the popular vote and a massive majority of seats in the Alberta legislature, ensuring a tenure of at least four years.

Notley was born in 1964, into one of the rarest things in Alberta: an NDP household. Her father, Grant Notley, had devoted himself to advancing socialism in Alberta, leading the Alberta New Democratic Party from 1968 until 1984, when he was killed tragically in a plane crash. He maintained a seat in the legislative assembly of Alberta from 1971 to 1984 — often as the only NDP member. He spent those years advocating for the interests of labour and social welfare in the face of overwhelming Conservative majorities. Rachel Notley's mother, born Sandra Mary Wilkinson, was an American political activist in the 1960s before settling in Alberta. Throughout her formative years, Rachel Notley was steeped in social activism and the New Democratic Party.

After graduating from Osgoode Hall Law School in the early 1990s, she returned to Alberta to practise labour law, and then moved to British Columbia in the mid-1990s to work with various NDP administrations and public sector unions. She returned again to Alberta in 2002, and eventually entered provincial politics in 2006. Notley was first elected in 2008, in Edmonton Strathcona, one of the few consistently NDP seats in the province. On October 18, 2014, Notley won the leadership of the Alberta NDP with 70 percent of the vote.

Leading up to the 2015 election, Notley focused primarily on social issues and spending priorities, not on climate policy or on market access for Alberta hydrocarbons. Her most significant public position on resource development was that KXL undermined Alberta's fundamental interest in maximizing upgrading and refining capacity within the province, citing "the export of forty thousand jobs to the U.S." Even worse, she aligned herself with the Northern Gateway project's opponents. Her position on KXL suggested a fundamental antipathy to corporate decision-making on maximizing return from Alberta's oil sands production. She was unprepared to trust industry's expertise on the realities of North American refinery optimization. Her lack of support for Northern Gateway, meanwhile, was simply inexplicable. She dismissed a viable option to deal with Alberta's urgent need for market access and questioned the integrity and professionalism of the Canadian regulatory process that had recommended the project's approval.

Notley was very much part of the national NDP establishment, at least until May 2015. Between 2000 and 2014 she had evolved as a champion of those elements in Alberta who were fundamentally alienated from the hydrocarbon industry and from the provincial governments that enabled massive investment in that industry. Little in Notley's biography prior to 2015 suggests that she sought alignment or accommodation with Alberta's corporate interests. But hers was not a life of privilege, unlike that of Justin Trudeau. She had no trust-fund legacy, and she and her husband supported their family primarily by working in the Alberta labour movement, with no part in the wealth associated with corporate or entrepreneurial Alberta. Authentic empathy for less affluent Albertans was natural for her. Of course, the political ethos of Alberta had never been defined by a belief in the redistribution of wealth; rather, the province's culture is imbued with a faith that virtually all Albertans can choose to prosper directly or indirectly from a growing private sector driven by the hydrocarbon production industry. Alberta was not Manitoba, let alone central Canada. The province more closely resembled a Texas with gun control and socialized medicine. This ethos rendered the Alberta NDP largely irrelevant — at least until May 2015.

Notley's 2015 campaign had virtually nothing to do with carbon or market access, nor did she even acknowledge the economic significance of Alberta's hydrocarbon production industry. Rather, Notley's rhetoric was consumed with restoring proposed cuts to education, health, and transportation spending. She rejected the grim austerity that the incumbent Jim Prentice claimed was Alberta's only possible response to the year-long collapse in oil prices and its resulting negative effect on provincial revenues.

If Trudeau was transparent in 2015 about his advocacy of carbon pricing, Notley, to the extent that she discussed carbon policy at all, ran on an official NDP position. It was based on three specifics: a phase-out of coal in electric generation; ending carbon-capture-and-sequestration pilots and redirecting that funding to public transit; and "leadership on climate," which meant crafting an unspecified solution while working with stakeholders and other governments. She emphasized energy efficiency and renewables, but she did not mention emissions reduction targets, carbon pricing, or specific sectoral emissions limits. Nor did she discuss market access.[19]

Of course, Notley also ran on a pledge to review Alberta's royalty policy, ensuring Albertans a "fairer share" and providing more incentives for industrial diversification. Just as predictably, she promised higher corporate and personal income taxes, and deficit spending. Incredibly, just a few days before the election, Notley came out publicly against Northern Gateway, contending that the project faced too much environmental and Indigenous resistance. Still, on May 5 Alberta elected Notley premier. To be fair, her opponent Jim Prentice offered nothing substantial on Alberta carbon policy either. He only defended the status quo; that is, Alberta's levy on larger industrial emitters. He made no suggestion that a new, more progressive carbon policy might be required to resolve Alberta's market access frustrations.

Support for the Progressive Conservative Party, which had controlled Alberta for more than five decades, melted away during the course of the election campaign and declined sharply after the leaders' debate. Prentice did not successfully make the case for austerity, and he did not convince Albertans that his government deserved another mandate to execute such a program.

After he left the Harper government in 2010, Prentice had joined the private sector. In 2014 Alberta's PC party insiders recruited him back into politics, essentially to salvage the party's electoral prospects after the debacles of Alison Redford's and Ed Stelmach's tenures as premier. As a

Harper Cabinet minister, Prentice had distinguished himself as a more genuinely progressive Conservative, at least in relative terms, though he had not managed to bend Harper's carbon policy toward a serious consideration of carbon taxes.

Prentice was premier of Alberta for roughly eight months, from September 2014 to May 2015, a period dominated by collapsing oil prices and market access frustrations, but also typified by unforced political misjudgments — most notably a botched effort to unify the two right-wing parties and Prentice's decision to hold an election in the spring of 2015. Clearly, he misread his government's electoral prospects. How would the province's carbon policy have evolved if Prentice had won the 2015 election or simply avoided an election entirely that year? Prentice appreciated the real challenges of finding a credible carbon policy for Alberta, one that would render powerless the national centre-left resentments over existing Alberta carbon and hydrocarbon development policy. Would Prentice have endorsed carbon taxes in Alberta? Perhaps, but he did not run on that position. Immediately after his defeat, he resigned from politics, and the province lost his reasonable centrist voice in the public discourse.

As mentioned earlier, Notley benefited in the 2015 election from two right-wing parties splitting the non-NDP vote. This was decisive in various Calgary and exurban Edmonton constituencies. Other factors helped Notley, such as the collapse of the Alberta Liberal Party's vote, continued population growth that provided the prospect of more progressive voters, and the resentments accumulated over almost forty-five years of PC rule. The result was an unassailable mandate for Notley, with fifty-four of eighty-four seats in place for at least the next four years.

Soon after her election, Notley appointed Brian Topp as her chief of staff. He was a long-time federal NDP player who spent his formative years working in Montreal-area politics and then moved on to Saskatchewan NDP governments for most of the 1990s. He held leadership positions in virtually every federal NDP campaign until he contended for the party's leadership in 2012, after the death of Jack Layton. Topp ran as a legitimate champion of traditional NDP policy, calling his opponent Thomas Mulcair too centrist. Of course, Mulcair, a Quebec

MP and former Quebec environment minister, prevailed, but Topp was endorsed by Rachel Notley, then a member of the Alberta provincial legislature.

Notley had Topp run her 2015 campaign despite his leadership role in the British Columbia NDP's failed 2013 campaign, which had opposed Kinder Morgan's Trans Mountain expansion project in a vain attempt to win support. Surely, a man who had opposed TMX, and who had no prior experience or affiliation with Alberta, was a strange choice to advocate for the interests of Albertans. After all, during his 2012 federal campaign he had put forward a plan that explicitly urged Canada to "forge a pan-Canada strategy to limit the environmental impacts of the oil sands. This includes the creation of a green investment fund, ending continental pipeline projects, like Keystone XL...."[20] Clearly, then, it was NDP credibility that was the key criterion for senior staff positions in the Notley government. Topp served as Notley's chief of staff for the decisive months of 2015 following her election through to the end of 2016. Like so many players I have already discussed, Topp had no real connection to, or history with, Alberta prior to the 2015 NDP election victory.

In June 2015 the Notley government announced that a panel headed by University of Alberta economics professor Andrew Leach would provide a new provincial carbon policy framework. On the same day, the province announced that it would be raising its carbon levy on large industrial emitters — it would increase from $15 per tonne to $30 per tonne by 2017. Fundamental change in carbon policy was at hand. Concurrently, Notley initiated a review of the province's fiscal position by former Bank of Canada governor and deputy minister of finance David Dodge. She also launched a long-promised review of provincial royalties. Dodge was there essentially to rationalize deficit spending, and he dutifully delivered in a strategic plan in October 2015.

The royalty review panel advised against fundamental change, citing massive declines in industry cash flow due to declining commodity prices, as well as continuing discounts due to inadequate market access infrastructure. To her credit, Notley substantially accepted these recommendations. Undoubtedly, Notley and Topp appreciated that Alberta required long-term growth in revenues from hydrocarbons to avoid even more difficult political trade-offs. The province needed a fundamental breakthrough on market access or it stood to lose billions of dollars of value per year. They clearly believed that Alberta needed a more credible carbon policy to achieve any such long-term breakthrough on market access, though the Notley government never, in 2015, made that linkage explicit.

Notley found herself in a troubling political context as the 2015 federal election unfolded. The federal NDP led the polls in early 2015, thanks, some argued, to uncharacteristically centrist policy positions, especially on fiscal responsibility. Certainly, the party's climate and energy policy positions remained as far left as ever. Mulcair supported no oil sands export projects, and clearly believed that climate change justified extremism, regardless of the economic consequences to Alberta and Canada. Mulcair vilified KXL as an export pipeline of Canadian jobs, and insisted that TMX required reassessment. He voiced no support for Energy East, regardless of its secure supply and economic impact. He denigrated the existing regulatory process, insisting that it was illegitimate because it failed to consider attributable carbon impacts. He advocated for more stringent emissions reduction targets for Canada, beyond the virtually impossible ones that Harper had already committed to coming out of Copenhagen, and he wanted them embedded in a national cap-and-trade system. Finally, he failed to disavow comments by Linda McQuaig, a star NDP candidate who insisted the Alberta oil sands resource needed to "stay in the ground." Needless to say, Mulcair did not advocate accommodation for Alberta's market access agenda. The federal NDP platform was in no way binding on the Alberta premier, but its ideas did represent the mindset of core NDP voters nationally.

Ultimately, we must credit people with what they actually do, rather than dwell on their former positions. Once the NDP was elected in Alberta, Topp and Notley became accountable to Albertans and their short- and long-term interests. In late November, just before the Paris climate conference commenced, the Notley government released both the Leach panel report and the actual Alberta climate policy document.[21] The two documents were distinct in significant ways, and both deserve credit for defining Alberta's climate policy primarily in terms of carbon pricing via a transparent and reasonably stringent carbon tax rather than in terms of overall emissions reduction targets. Alberta would internalize climate risk through pricing, and it would expect in return that the rest of Canada recognize — if grudgingly — that the province had established a credible carbon policy. Doubtlessly, Leach must have spent many hours persuading the Notley government that carbon pricing was the appropriate Alberta policy, and that more direct regulation would only contract Alberta's economy.

Alberta's carbon policy contained the following key specifics:

1. An economy-wide carbon tax. Albertans would be subject to an economy-wide carbon tax of $20 per tonne beginning in January 2017, to grow to $30 per tonne by January 2018. The proceeds of this carbon tax would remain in Alberta, to be spent by the provincial government on advancing green technology, to offset the regressive aspects of the tax, and to deal with competitiveness issues for Alberta's energy-intensive, trade-exposed sectors. Initially, the carbon tax proceeds were not to fund existing operations of the Alberta government. How the tax increased with time was at the discretion of the government. The tax was not revenue neutral to Alberta taxpayers. It was an additional tax.

2. Accelerated phasing out of coal, and greater reliance on renewable power sources. Alberta would phase out coal-fired electricity production by 2030, and renewable energy sources would comprise approximately 30 percent of Alberta's electricity production by 2030.

3. An absolute limit on carbon emissions from oil sands production. The policy set a limit of 100 MT per year. The existing base in 2015 was approximately 70 MT per year. There was no specific guidance on how the cap would be allocated to prospective or existing oil sands producers. This was not recommended by the Leach panel, but added by the Notley government on its own, as a key adjunct to the recommendations.

4. Implementation of a new methane-emissions reduction strategy. The goal was 45 percent of 2014 levels by 2025. The policy did not clarify how or at what cost to competitiveness this would be achieved.

Both the oil sands emissions cap and the accelerated coal phase-out were utterly inconsistent with a carbon policy premised on carbon pricing as the pre-eminent policy instrument. One emission has no more impact than another, but in these two sectors, emissions beyond a certain date or a certain threshold would be taxed de facto at infinity. Nevertheless, the Notley government believed it must provide physical reductions from Alberta by 2030 regardless of the cost, even if she put no direct limit on hydrocarbon production.

The cost to Albertans of the coal phase-out was not laid out with the policy's release, nor was it clarified subsequently. But, incredibly, Albertans would have to pay out existing coal generation and then endure overall higher generation costs than would have been obtained if the coal operators had merely paid the going carbon tax of $30 per tonne. The same applied in respect to the oil sands emissions cap. It ignored whether Alberta oil sands production was viable enough to afford the carbon tax, failing to account for the opportunity costs to Alberta, and simply imposed an absolute prohibition after the specific limit of 100 MT per year attributed to oil sands production. Worst of all, neither the Leach report nor the ultimate government policy made the plan contingent on resolving Alberta's market access demands. This failure would haunt the Notley government over time, as Albertans consistently asked what they got for this new tax. According to the Notley government, its climate plan restored policy credibility to Alberta, which would implicitly provide sufficient social licence for market access.

Essentially, Notley chose simply to impose carbon taxes first, along with two serious and unnecessary interventions in the Alberta energy sector — accelerated coal shutdown, and an emissions cap — without offering Albertans anything tangible in return, in terms of market access assurances from the federal government. Four major oil sands operators, including the three largest Canadian-owned entities, explicitly endorsed the Notley climate plan, with the oil sands emissions cap. The hydrocarbon production industry, as represented by the Canadian Association of Petroleum Producers (CAPP), never endorsed it explicitly, although there may have been potential for broader acceptance of carbon taxes under a different set of policy terms than was contained in the Notley climate plan. The motivations of those four operators for acceding to the oil sands emissions cap remains inexplicable, given their corporate imperative for rational, long-term carbon policy based on transparent, revenue-neutral carbon taxes. Perhaps they simply believed the Notley regime would go down soon enough, before the emissions cap became a practical constraint. Some may have rationalized the cap as consistent with the likely increase in oil sands production by 2030, an aggregate level of four million barrels per day, absent any technological breakthrough that reduced the extraction process's carbon intensity. That view also relied on assumptions about future global commodity and carbon pricing.

As for the ENGOs, they acknowledged that Alberta's carbon pricing was constructive, but they conceded nothing on market access, supporting no specific oil sands export project; they maintained their fundamental antipathy to oil sands production. Of course, no ENGO would make the trade. A carbon tax of $30 per tonne may be enough to accelerate the phase-out of some coal capacity, but it could never materially impact oil sands economics or hydrocarbon consumption economics. Even with this tax, as stringent as any American or European cap-and-trade scheme up to that point, it was delusional to expect it to be sufficient to achieve ENGO acquiescence for oil sands market access.

DECEMBER IN PARIS, 2015

Just three days after the 2015 federal election, Gerald Butts, Brian Topp, and Andrew Leach met in Ottawa. Alberta was to disclose to the new Trudeau government the key elements of its as-yet-undisclosed climate plan. Would the plan prove palatable enough, especially on the cusp of the Paris climate meeting, which was just six weeks away? Would even an Alberta NDP government fail to deliver adequate climate policy for the province? Trudeau and Butts should not have worried. The Alberta plan, as represented by the Leach panel report, was staunchly committed to credible carbon pricing, accelerated coal phase-out, and stronger methane-emissions regulations. The cap on oil sands production was still under negotiation between Alberta ENGOs and a subset of Alberta oil sands producers. Any breakthrough would only add to the palatability of the Alberta plan — and in fact a breakthrough did occur, in the form of a cap based on emissions instead of production, albeit (as we have seen) with the public acquiescence of only four oil sands operators. Not surprisingly, four weeks later Trudeau enthusiastically endorsed the Notley climate plan as a "very positive step in the fight against climate change."

Neither Trudeau's government, nor Notley's, commented publicly on market access in the run-up to Paris; however, that October 19 meeting left TMX and Energy East as the only remaining options. Trudeau and Notley both conceded that Obama's formal rejection of KXL was imminent, and both had already long since dismissed Northern Gateway. Energy East had barely commenced its regulatory process in 2015, and any decision was likely two or three years away. TMX, then, required a decision, likely within the next year. Notley needed an affirmative decision on TMX to sustain her political position, a point not lost on Topp or Butts.

Days after the Alberta climate plan was disclosed, Canada's first ministers — the provincial and territorial premiers, along with the prime minister — convened in Ottawa to coordinate the Canadian delegation at the Paris climate conference, which they would all attend. At that meeting the ministers agreed on no national climate plan. They found no consensus on carbon pricing, notwithstanding the breakthrough in Alberta's position. They did not discuss market access. But Canada had its national targets, established by the Harper government in May 2015 and appropriated by Trudeau: by 2030 Canada would cut its emissions by 30 percent from 2005 levels. The commitment to meet those emissions reduction targets was the core of Canada's contribution to Paris. Of course, there was no public disclosure on the specifics of how to meet those targets. Nevertheless, those assembled leaders felt Alberta had sufficiently rehabilitated itself with its new climate policy. As a result, the opprobrium Canada had endured from the international community in 2009 in Copenhagen would be mitigated, if not entirely eliminated.

The Paris Climate Accord came together with the following key points for Canada:

1. Countries committed to keeping the rise in global temperatures below 2 degrees Celsius, a level beyond which scientists predict possible

catastrophic consequences. Countries set a 1.5 degree rise as an aspirational goal. Canada pledged to cut its emissions by 30 percent from 2005 levels by 2030.

2. Specific emissions reductions are not legally binding on nations, but nations must monitor and report emissions. Countries would meet every five years to review progress.

3. Developed countries committed to spending at least $100 billion per year between 2020 and 2025 to help emerging economies deal with the effects of climate change.[22]

Trudeau glibly conveyed to the conference that Canada "will take on a new leadership role internationally." As for Canada's targets, he conceded, "We know that we have work to do," and further opined that "carbon pricing — be it through a carbon tax or a cap-and-trade system — is a crucial tool to begin the shift we need towards sustainable economic growth."

But the end of 2015 was a euphoric moment for both Trudeau and Notley, two soulmates of progressive public policy; they were confident that they had squared the circle of climate credibility while abiding just enough growth in Alberta hydrocarbons and related infrastructure.

CHAPTER 2

2016: Incoherence and Contradictions

AS FOR RATIONALIZING CANADA'S CLIMATE and hydrocarbon dilemma, 2016 was defined by decisions on pipelines, including two apparent approvals, the fortuitous revival of KXL, the formal ratification of Canada's participation in the Paris Climate Accord, and a new federal climate policy. This new climate policy, the Pan-Canadian Framework on Clean Growth and Climate Change, was based substantially on carbon pricing, and it achieved acceptance, if not support, from most of the provincial governments. But the net result was continued incoherence.

In March 2016, following through on his commitment of November 2015, Trudeau convened the provincial premiers in Vancouver to seek consensus on a strategy to meet Canada's emissions reduction target as per the Paris Accord. Two of the more prominent figures at this meeting were federal energy minister Jim Carr and federal environment minister Catherine McKenna. Carr, a long-time Liberal politician, had recently led the Business Council of Manitoba, where he worked prominently on energy and carbon policy issues until he was elected to Parliament in 2015. He had, however, no direct experience in energy-related industries. McKenna, a lawyer in her midforties, was first elected in 2015 as well, and represented an inner city Ottawa constituency. Her law practice had focused on competition, trade, and constitutional law, not regulatory

Natural Resources Minister Jim Carr arrives for a meeting about TMX.

Prime Minister Justin Trudeau hugs Catherine McKenna at her swearing-in as environment and climate change minister, November 2015.

or environmental law. Working alongside the prime minister, this pair would be the major public spokespeople for the federal government's energy and climate policy, though their contributions were constrained by the dictates of the Prime Minister's Office.

McKenna was an intense, earnest advocate for Canada's meeting its environmental commitments, if not exceeding them, but would not cross the line by directly opposing specific pipeline or LNG development projects. She carried the greatest burden after Trudeau himself to show that Canada was credible on achieving emissions reduction targets. Despite his role as de facto advocate for Canadian resource industries, Carr was always all in on Canada's Paris commitments, without any apparent equivocation. Neither of them had anything to offer on the costs of compliance or on rationalizing growing hydrocarbon production to meet the Paris targets.

At Vancouver, Trudeau and Notley were like soulmates, both making the case that carbon pricing was indispensable for Canada to achieve climate policy credibility, to demonstrate to Canadian and international critics that the country was doing its part to contribute to dealing with the risk of climate change even as it continued the development of the greenhouse gas–intensive oil sands sector. Market access, however, was another issue. The best Notley could muster from the other premiers was a statement that "all premiers agreed this was a matter that needs to be dealt with on an urgent basis."[1] She received no concessions from British Columbia or Quebec on specific issues related to TMX, Northern Gateway, and Energy East, let alone overall conceptual support for those projects; nor did the provinces relent on specific conditions required for such support.[2]

In the communiqué that came out of this meeting, the premiers committed to "transition to a low carbon economy by adopting a broad range of domestic measures, including carbon-pricing mechanisms, adapted to each province's and territory's specific circumstance," all in the context of meeting Canada's 2030 emissions reduction targets coming out of the Paris conference. This statement was contested by Progressive Conservative premier Brad Wall of Saskatchewan, who objected to carbon pricing unequivocally. No other provincial premier explicitly opposed carbon pricing in concept. But none publicly raised the question of what compliance would cost Canada, or how that cost would compare with what Canada's major trading partners were imposing on themselves. The ministers delegated bureaucratic working groups to spend six months studying four key elements of what would eventually become national climate strategy: the specifics of carbon pricing design; other measures to reduce emissions; development and adoption of clean technology; and helping communities adapt to the impacts of climate change.

Unfortunately for Albertans, Notley did not insist publicly on an explicit quid pro quo from Ottawa in return for a progressive carbon policy from Alberta. She had already acquiesced to the Trudeau government's assault on the Northern Gateway project. Even before she rolled out her climate plan in mid-November 2015, Trudeau had directed Transport Minister Marc Garneau to impose a moratorium on crude oil tanker traffic off British Columbia's north coast. The moratorium served one only short-run purpose — namely, to disable the Northern Gateway project. The whole point was clearly to undermine the permit Harper's government had granted, even as Enbridge diligently worked to meet the NEB's imposed conditions, including to maximize Indigenous alignment.

The NEB had dealt with the issue of tanker safety, impacts to the area proximate to Kitimat, and related emergency response in a regulatory process it fairly described as "one of the most exhaustive reviews of its kind in Canadian history." The proponents, Enbridge and its shippers, held out the naïve hope they could negotiate with the Trudeau government and salvage the pipeline. This direct, large-scale pipeline project was designed to carry diluted bitumen from Edmonton to Kitimat, providing direct tidewater access at a scale close to that offered by KXL, roughly 800,000 barrels per day. It was fully supported by prospective shippers, a mix of oil sands producers, and Asian refining interests, and offered a potential capital investment exceeding $10 billion. From the project's first disclosure in 2008, it faced bitter resistance from Canadian ENGOs and certain First Nations proximate to the Kitimat terminal. This opposition continued throughout the regulatory process until that was finalized early in 2012. Key among the opponents was WWF Canada, led by Gerry Butts through most of that time period.

Notley acquiesced in the tanker ban instead of condemning it as unfair to Alberta. Enbridge was in a position to launch legal action against the federal government on the premise that the ban's only purpose was to nullify its Northern Gateway project; at a minimum, compensation for costs would be on the order of half a billion dollars. For reasons that remain unknown, however, Enbridge did not pursue litigation. The Trudeau government cautiously moved forward with legislation to implement the tanker ban.

In May 2016 the NEB recommended approval of TMX. The government had by statute seven months to make a decision on the recommendation, which contained 157 conditions, including 49 environmental requirements.[3] As in the case of Northern Gateway, the NEB concluded that the project would provide economic advantages for Canada, including access to export markets, thousands of construction jobs, and increased government revenue. Moreover, it judged the probability of a major oil spill as sufficiently low to justify approval. The NEB chose to exceed its jurisdiction related to both the pipeline and the terminal to consider possible environmental effects of additional tanker shipping attributable to the advent of TMX, but it did not ultimately apply any conditions to such additional shipping, leaving that to other federal entities that had specific statutory authority for such regulation. This NEB decision to eschew conditions on tanker traffic would prove especially problematic in 2018, when, as a result of an intervention by the Federal Court of Appeal, the apparent approval of the project was undone. At the time of the NEB's decision, reaction was predictable, with Alberta and the oil industry expressing relief and support for it and the ENGO community castigating it, arguing it was impossible to "build more pipelines and meet the international climate commitments that Canada agreed to in Paris."[4] But TMX, as the option that Trudeau and Notley had implicitly agreed upon, was moving forward as expected and as required.

The following month, the Federal Court of Appeal set back market access for the Northern Gateway project in its decision in *Gitxaala Nation v. Canada*. In a two-to-one split decision, the court ruled the government's Indigenous consultation framework inadequate, that it "fell well short of the mark." The court's decision overturned the federal Cabinet's June

2014 approval of Enbridge's Northern Gateway pipeline. This ruling set a precedent that would brutally impact TMX, Trudeau, and Notley in 2018. The court quashed the order-in-council, nullifying the NEB certificates that approved Northern Gateway. The matter was sent back to Cabinet for redetermination, giving Trudeau the opportunity to in effect approve or not approve Northern Gateway by deciding to remedy or not to remedy the faults identified in the court's decision.

According to the court, the deficiency in consultation related exclusively to the period after the NEB had recommended approval and before the federal Cabinet explicitly endorsed it — all of which was roughly five years after the regulatory process commenced. The court found no deficiencies on the part of Enbridge or the NEB itself, but rather on the part of the federal Cabinet, the final decision-maker. The majority decision held that the consultation was not "meaningful" enough: the officials who engaged in the consultation on behalf of Cabinet were not sufficiently empowered, and the consultation amounted merely to noting grievances.

First Nations, the court stated, were entitled to "more," meaning, presumably, further negotiation to find accommodation on outstanding grievances. In contrast, the dissenting member of the Federal Court of Appeal held that any imperfections in the Crown's consultations were insufficient to amount to inadequacy — in other words, the standard for consulting is adequacy, not perfection. In any case, the fact was that re-establishing Northern Gateway's approval would require redoing the last phase of the consultation. Regardless of how the crude oil ban played out in the courts vis-à-vis Northern Gateway, this appeal court decision was a gift to Trudeau. It allowed him to end the project simply by doing nothing, instead of by trying to remedy the Federal Court of Appeal's cited deficiency. The fate of Northern Gateway was directly in his hands, with no need for the indirection of tanker bans.

Still, the court had set a standard — a standard the Trudeau government would have to respect if it intended to approve TMX and insure it against future appeals. The Trudeau government chose three initiatives to better validate its inevitable TMX approval. First, it commissioned an Environment Canada analysis of upstream greenhouse gas emissions associated with the project, to better understand its climate impacts. Second, the Government of Canada recommitted to ongoing consultation with First Nations whose interests would be affected by the pipeline's construction and operation. And third, on May 17, 2016, Minister of Natural Resources Carr announced the appointment of a three-member panel to complement the NEB review and identify gaps and/or issues of concern for the government to consider before deciding the fate of the pipeline proposal.

The Environment Canada analysis attributed to TMX maximum emissions of roughly 15 MT annually, assuming that all of the barrels it carried were incremental. Remember, the national challenge was to reduce emissions by more than 200 MT annually by 2030. The report did not offer any guidance on how TMX and that target would relate to each other.[5] As for the special panel created by Carr, its report focused on the basic contradiction of any additional oil sands project: How could Canada reconcile hydrocarbon development with its emissions reduction targets? The report reiterated the fundamental critiques made by those implacably opposed to the project, highlighting, in particular, Canada's obligations under the United Nations Declaration on the Rights of Indigenous Peoples to proceed with resource development consistent with the standard of the "free, prior and informed consent of the indigenous peoples" with relevant land claims.

The report conveyed that the feedback it received from Alberta respondents was almost diametrically opposite to that received in British Columbia. This was hardly a revelation, but it confirmed the divide between those whose livelihood was tied to oil sands production and those implacably opposed to the entire proposition in the context of the climate change risk. The panel only validated what the NEB record already showed — that TMX was economically necessary, especially to Alberta, notwithstanding that it would increase the challenge of achieving national emissions reductions.

Direct consultation between government officials and Indigenous groups continued, as required by the Federal Court of Appeal. Somewhat incredibly, this consultation still amounted to acknowledging grievances and even implacable opposition, but was never documented as less than genuine negotiation.

• • • • •

In October 2016 the Trudeau government moved to formally ratify Canada's Paris commitment by a vote of the Canadian parliament, which meant the country was bound to "meet or exceed" greenhouse gas emissions reductions by 30 percent from 2005 levels by 2030, in the context of a collective commitment to limit the rise in average global temperatures to less than 2 degrees Celsius above preindustrial levels, with an aim of less than 1.5 degrees. Legally, Canada was committed merely to reporting its progress toward those targets, but Carr encapsulated the Trudeau government's mindset with his comments, which revealed unnuanced aspiration coupled with limited clarity on implementation or cost:

> The Paris agreement highlights the urgency of our environmental responsibility while pointing us toward new economic opportunities.
>
> It speaks to the necessity of co-operation toward a common goal. The agreement also reflects a compelling reality that while the transition to a lower-carbon future might be long, the trajectory is clear. We simply cannot continue along the present course.[6]

To meet the commitments that Canada made in Paris, the Trudeau government decided that a tax on carbon was necessary. If certain premiers refused to enact legislation to help achieve that goal, Ottawa would impose a tax of $10 per tonne, rising to $50 per tonne in 2022, the equivalent of eleven cents per litre at the pump. This was the minimum ante expected of the Canadian provinces, and it conformed to Alberta's lead of the year before. Each province had a deadline of September 1, 2018, to establish how it would implement the federal standard.

Meanwhile, Alberta diligently implemented non-pricing elements of its climate plan, most notably its accelerated coal shutdown provisions, related renewable mandates, and carbon taxes across the province's economy. Twelve of eighteen coal-fired power plants were already required by Harper-era federal regulations to shut down by 2030, but Alberta would still have to pay $1.36 billion by 2030 to private sector owners of coal-generation infrastructure, to compensate for lost value. Alberta also committed itself to 30 percent wind, solar, and hydro by 2030, with specific contracts for the initial tranches of such capacity to be awarded in 2017. On June 7, 2016, Alberta's Bill 20, the Climate Leadership Implementation Act (CLIA), passed its third reading in the legislature. CLIA allowed for a carbon tax on Alberta's industry and citizens, which came into effect January 1, 2017. The Notley government never put into context how much these initiatives on coal shutdown and renewables would cost Albertans relative to the federal $30 per tonne carbon tax benchmark. Nor did it spell out what level of carbon tax would have seen the shutdowns and generation selections occur because they made sense economically for the private sector, rather than by mandate and edict.

Late in 2016, all of this culminated in decisions on pipelines. The federal Liberal government formally approved both Kinder Morgan Canada's plan to expand its Trans Mountain pipeline system and Enbridge's Line 3 replacement project, which provide additional capacity of approximately three hundred thousand barrels per day to U.S. markets. At the same time, Trudeau announced that the government would not approve Enbridge's Northern Gateway project, and that Ottawa would impose a ban on oil tanker traffic on the northern section of British Columbia's west coast. At his November 29 press conference, Trudeau offered no more than a quip to justify his denial of Northern Gateway: "The Great Bear Rainforest is no place for a pipeline, and the Douglas Channel is no place for oil tanker traffic." In his remarks on the Northern Gateway project, he made no reference to the multiyear regulatory process that had recommended approval for it, and failed to mention the fact that, despite the Federal Court of Appeal ruling in the matter, the government had made no attempts to remedy the deficiencies in consultation identified by the court.

* * * * *

Notley had nothing to say about the loss of Northern Gateway. Instead, she extolled the two projects that had been approved, calling them "morning light" after "a long dark night" of low commodity prices and frustration on market access. She added that the Alberta government would conform its carbon pricing to the federal standard, $50 per tonne by 2022 — in full alignment with federal carbon policy.

Predictably, the Canadian ENGO community, along with some First Nations, most notably the Tsleil-Waututh Nation resident at Burrard Inlet, were bitterly disappointed, vowing both litigation and civil disobedience. They accused Trudeau of betrayal and political opportunism, although they shouldn't have been surprised by his decision. Against all logic, Trudeau continued to contend that his approvals would not compromise Canada's ability to meet its climate change targets, even though he offered no quantified explanation of how that could be. This was enraging to the ENGO movement, but what they especially resented was the fact that the TMX regulatory process had deemed attributable carbon effects to be outside its scope, deferring instead to the government in deciding on how to deal with the issue.

Concern over carbon effects are at the core the ENGO community's opposition to the pipeline, notwithstanding its long-standing contention that TMX should be rejected in any case, due to the special spill risks of diluted bitumen, impacts on killer whales in Burrard Inlet, and insufficient Indigenous accommodation. How could a government purportedly committed to meeting its Paris targets rationalize an approval for a project that would enable an incremental increase in emissions?

The government's response to that question was the Pan-Canadian Framework on Clean Growth and Climate Change. The framework was finalized on December 9, 2016, at a climate-focused first ministers' meeting in Ottawa. Its key element was carbon pricing. According to a federal benchmark, provincial and territorial governments would implement the price, starting at $10 per tonne in 2018, and then increase it by $10 each year until it reached $50 per tonne in 2022. The document also committed Canada to developing new building codes to ensure that buildings used less energy; to deploying more electric charging stations to support zero-emitting vehicles; to expanding clean electricity systems; to promoting inter-ties (infrastructure to move more electricity across provinces); to using smart-grid technologies to better balance real-time supply and demand of electricity, which helps to phase out reliance on coal as a source of electricity generation; to making more efficient use of existing power supplies; to ensuring a greater use of renewable energy; and to reducing methane leakages. The formal document included a bar chart that showed estimated reductions from provincial and federal plans to date (including carbon offsets/credits); carbon pricing standards; and other new initiatives cited in the document, notably coal phase-out, but with a gap of forty-four million tonnes to be filled by "additional measures." These numbers implicitly offered projections of national economic growth, hydrocarbon production, additional hydrocarbon infrastructure, and the applicability of the Alberta oil sands emissions cap. The document did not specify how this bar chart was derived.[7]

Soon after its release, critics would question the Pan-Canadian Framework's ability to sufficiently reduce emissions, but at the end of 2016 it was in place and accepted by the majority of provinces, with the vague promise to do more, if necessary, to meet the Paris targets. Trudeau could not, however, persuade Saskatchewan to accept the central tenet. Premier Wall consistently refused any form of carbon pricing, emphasizing that it would merely add cost to an economically challenged production sector without materially affecting carbon emissions. Wall did not offer an alternative vision of credible climate change policy, but he rejected participating in the Pan-Canadian Framework and planned to resist on constitutional grounds federal efforts to impose carbon pricing on Saskatchewan. Manitoba's premier Brian Pallister did not sign on either, but not because of his government's stance on climate and energy policy; rather, he wanted increased federal health care funding for Manitoba, and tried to use the framework as leverage. Although British Columbia, then led by Liberal Christy Clark, emphasized that all the provinces must apply the same stringency of carbon pricing, and feared that some would equivocate or evade the national standard using complex cap-and-trade design, she did join. Seven provinces endorsed the Pan-Canadian Framework.

Notley, of course, was all in. Throughout the deliberations on December 9, she fully supported the federal position as articulated in the framework. Her quid pro quo was, apparently, being honoured. But as well, by the end of 2016, the unexpected election of Donald Trump occurred, portending the potential reversal of American federal carbon policy and a revived KXL.

The Pan-Canadian Framework on Clean Growth and Climate Change remained McKenna's cross to bear for the next several years. As genuinely committed as she was to achieve the Paris targets, she carried the burden of trying to rationalize oil sands infrastructure and LNG production. The ENGO community eventually called for her resignation, while Trudeau himself faced the same condemnation for the incoherence of the Canadian position on climate.[8] But Canada still had close to fourteen years to meet its target — why worry?

CHAPTER 3

2017: Revivals and Lost Options

THE CANADIAN PUBLIC, according to certain national polls at the end of 2016, generally supported the Trudeau government's position on carbon pricing and market access as represented by the approvals of Line 3 and TMX. Canada apparently validated a quintessentially centrist position, despite significant regional differences. So, in 2017 there seemed general support for Liberal policies on carbon pricing, but it was recognized that overall support could well change once carbon pricing materially impacted Canadian households, and with the potential advent of other provincial governments more aligned with Saskatchewan's opposition to carbon pricing. However, the Trudeau government would not likely face that reaction in the short run. Predictably, 2017 did not bring any changes in government climate policy. But the year saw events unfold that exacerbated the country's internal divisions. For Alberta, progress on achieving market access confronted more obstacles, while the Canadian ENGO movement and other elements of the Canadian left remained skeptical that Trudeau's government would impose interventions necessary to realize Canada's Paris commitments.

Trudeau inflamed Alberta attitudes toward his government in early January 2017 at a town hall in Peterborough, Ontario, when he asserted that the country needs to "phase out Alberta tar sands production and make the transition away from fossil fuels." This sparked immediate reactions of incredulity from Alberta and the Canadian oil industry, so much that the PMO had to issue a statement that amounted less to a retraction than to careful sophistry:

> The prime minister — as he and previous prime ministers, including Stephen Harper, have been saying for a long time — was reiterating the need to move away from our dependency on fossil fuels and his commitment to growing the economy, all while protecting the environment. As a government, we were proud to work with provinces and territories to introduce a price on carbon pollution — to create jobs and protect the environment. We are also proud of our recent announcement which will ensure that we can move Canada's natural resources to international markets.

The official clarification did not ease many Albertans' doubts about the Trudeau government's commitment to the province's basic economic interests.

THE REVIVAL OF KXL

Within weeks of Donald Trump's inauguration as president of the United States, he launched a process to reverse the previous government's eight years of procrastination on and ultimate denial of KXL. This process culminated on March 24, 2017, with the issuance of a long-awaited permit to TransCanada CEO Russ Girling. The 800,000-plus-barrels-per-day, $8 billion-plus project was back in business.

KXL was as much an icon for the American right as it had become for the left, and any Republican president would have granted the permit. For Canada, Trump's reversal meant the largest, most economically rational of all of its market access options was back in play. One can

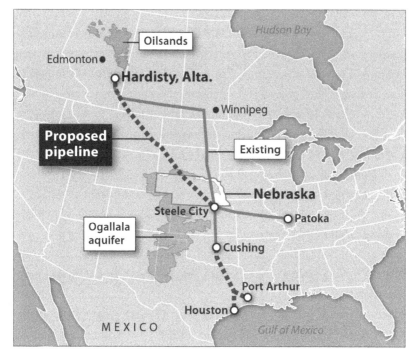

Source: TransCanada Pipelines LTD.; USGS; The Canadian Press
KXL Route

President Donald Trump in the Oval Office with TransCanada CEO Russell Girling (far left) after signing an order approving the development of KXL, March 2017.

only wonder what the Trudeau government would have done differently if it had anticipated Trump's win and a revival of KXL. Perhaps Trudeau would have stretched out the TMX process to avoid making an approval, notwithstanding the understanding struck with Notley. Admittedly, TMX provided Canadian tidewater access, which KXL could not. But the scale of KXL substantially resolved the market access issue for the short and medium term, regardless of the fate of any other market access option.

TransCanada still had serious hurdles to face before construction could commence. To reassemble the project, TransCanada needed to restore shipper support, reconvene the project team, recontract various service providers, and reorient its own capital allocation to this unexpected second chance. Most importantly, it had to contend with unfinished business in Nebraska, as the pipeline's route through that state had never been resolved. The governor's approval, granted in 2012, had been appealed as outside his authority and as a matter instead for the state's regulatory authority. Rather than relying on the 2012 approval, which the Nebraska Supreme Court had upheld in 2015, TransCanada decided that it would face less chance of long-term judicial obstruction if it also obtained an approval from the state regulatory commission for the same route and project design. Late in 2017, the Nebraska Public Utilities Commission did indeed approve a route through Nebraska. Though the approved route was not precisely the one TransCanada had applied for, the company deemed it close enough to justify sustaining the project. By a three-to-two decision, the route was altered from a crooked diagonal across the state to more of a right angle, following the existing base Keystone right of way south at the state's eastern border.

At long last, KXL had a route through Nebraska and a presidential permit. By the end of the year, TransCanada announced that it had restored its shipper base. It stopped short, however, of formally announcing a final investment decision to proceed, affirming only that it was progressing the project. TransCanada maintained a relatively low profile on KXL, only providing as much public disclosure as required and reacting to specific developments. Putting the project into service would, nevertheless, be of enormous consequence for the company financially and for Canadian oil sands producers, including the Alberta government. Predictably, a collection of Nebraska landowners launched a suit challenging the Nebraska Public Utilities Commission decision, and resolving this litigation consumed most of 2018. TransCanada demonstrated great caution, chastened by past experience of ramping up spending before all requisite approvals were in hand.

Alberta's Notley government and the federal Trudeau government showed no reservations about KXL's revival. Notley had previously mused that Alberta should build its own refineries for upgrading bitumen rather than exporting it through KXL to American refineries, but she set all that aside. The Alberta government even became a KXL shipper in order to move some of the royalty share that it would take in kind; cash flow from selling diluted bitumen volumes would be maximized through KXL, as compared to any market access alternative.

With this long-term shipping commitment on the order of twenty years, the Notley government showed that it accepted the economic realities of Alberta. Whatever Notley may have said about energy transition and "green" opportunities, she committed to a project that relied on enduring market demand for Alberta's diluted bitumen. Neither Trudeau nor Notley acknowledged that KXL would lead to greater upstream oil sands carbon emissions, making it more challenging for the country to meet its emissions reduction targets. From Trudeau's perspective, KXL posed none of the NIMBY issues that would afflict TMX and Energy East. The small portion of the project routed through Canada would run through Alberta, a province that would not object. Any continuing resistance would occur in the United States, and American governments would deal with it.

For the American ENGOs, KXL's revival was a bitter disappointment. With Trump as president and Republican congressional majorities in the House and the Senate, the ENGOs' only recourse if they hoped to stop the project was through the courts. Protests in Washington, D.C., or in Nebraska could not alter that reality. The American environmental movement could no longer rely on a fundamentally sympathetic Obama. Instead, they now faced their worst nightmare in terms of federal carbon and energy policy: an energy policy dictated by an unrepentant climate denier.

Leading figures from both American and Canadian ENGOs excoriated Trudeau and Notley for their decisions on market access. Bill McKibben, the activist who had led the successful movement to thwart KXL by applying political pressure on the Obama administration, called the Canadian prime minister a "disaster for the planet." He said Trudeau offered only comforting rhetoric on climate change while he failed to reduce, much less eliminate, oil sands production.

Especially intolerable for McKibben were Trudeau's remarks of early 2017 at the CERAWeek energy conference, hosted by Cambridge Energy Research Associates: "No country would find 173 billion barrels of oil in the ground and just leave them there."[1] As usual, McKibben was all in on the carbon math. Converting all 173 billion barrels into actual production, he stressed, would generate 30 percent of the total global carbon emissions required to exceed 1.5 degrees Celsius, the aspirational goal of the entire Paris Climate Accord. Canada, he concluded, represented one-half of 1 percent of the planet's population, but claimed the right to sell oil that would use up a third of the earth's remaining carbon budget. Trudeau, according to this logic, could not have been more hypocritical.

Canada's long-time environmentalist activist David Suzuki was just as harsh, in April 2017 describing Canadian actions on climate change as "disgusting," and not "serious about the promise made at Paris." Nothing short of reducing Canadian hydrocarbon production would assuage Suzuki, and he never acknowledged that Canada's carbon-pricing standard was actually more stringent than any price generated by its major trading partners thus far. However, the absurd expectations voiced by McKibben and Suzuki had no impact on existing approvals or on the Pan-Canadian Framework on Clean Growth and Climate Change.

Notley faced a similar rejection in the spring of 2016, at the national NDP convention in Edmonton where delegates supported in principle the *Leap Manifesto*, a political agenda conceived by leftist writers and activists Naomi Klein and Avi Lewis. The document called for Canadians to explicitly reject Alberta's primary industry, hydrocarbon production, and to deconstruct much of the existing Canadian private sector economy. The federal NDP, outside of Alberta, consequently aligned itself more closely with McKibben than with Notley, making no accommodation for the political and economic realities of Alberta. This left little doubt that Notley's real political soulmate was Justin Trudeau, not the federal NDP.

NORTHERN GATEWAY

After the Trudeau government formally rejected Northern Gateway in late 2016, the only question that remained was whether the project's proponents would consider any further appeals or litigation. The proponents certainly could make a legitimate claim that they had carried out their consultation obligations and participated fully in an arduous and thorough regulatory process — a process that had culminated in an actual approval. It would have been easy for the sponsors of the project to argue that their efforts were rendered pointless because the Trudeau government chose to simply not remedy the deficiencies cited in the Federal Court of Appeal ruling, which related solely to the inadequacy of the government's consultation in the latest stages of the approval process. The government had victimized those who acted in good faith, and left them with unrecovered costs of over half a billion dollars. This group included not only Enbridge and its shippers, but also thirty of the forty-two First

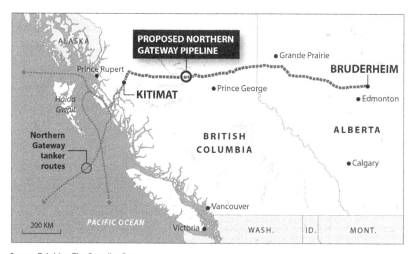

Source: Enbridge; The Canadian Press
Northern Gateway Route

Nations on the pipeline's right of way, who looked forward to sharing in the construction and long-term benefits. But Enbridge chose not to pursue any litigation in respect of how the Trudeau government rejected Northern Gateway. Perhaps if the court had not ruled against the existing approval, the tanker ban initiative would have been contested. In any case, Enbridge closed down the project over the first half of 2017, and Canada lost an option on market access that could have been completed well before the end of the decade.

Little has been published as a post mortem on the project from the perspective of the proponents. The project never successfully obtained any significant level of support, or even nominal acceptance, from First Nations on the coast near Kitimat (Enbridge had established agreements with many of the First Nations along the route from Edmonton), despite Enbridge's persistent efforts to find accommodation on potential spill risk mitigation and provision of a reasonable share of economic benefits arising from the project. Nevertheless, Enbridge chose to press on with the formal regulatory process despite that opposition, and the Harper government granted its approval as well.

A lingering question concerning the fate of the project remains: Why did it not move to construction before the 2015 federal election that brought Trudeau to power? It must be admitted that litigation risk was already in play when Harper granted the approval, and the project still needed to satisfy more than two hundred conditions; still, however, Enbridge could have formally requested from the NEB permission to commence construction based on the level of compliance with required conditions it had actually achieved, which was not unsubstantial. Furthermore, it could have challenged the federal government to provide requisite approvals to work around the B.C.'s government if the province held that its "five conditions" had not been adequately satisfied and therefore withheld normal course permits. But Enbridge never made that demand of the Harper government.

Doubtless, some of Harper's strategists preferred leaving Enbridge to meet the NEB's conditions and British Columbia's five conditions to reinforce the project's federal approval during the run-up to the 2015 federal election. But given all of the Harper government's previous rhetoric about Northern Gateway — how the project was self-evidently in the public interest, especially with the imminent loss of KXL — it remains puzzling that it was not more proactive in getting the project built. The same can be said of the project proponents themselves. Northern Gateway had complied with the formal regulatory process and gained approval on the basis that it was deemed in the national interest. Since it was a project under federal jurisdiction, one might have expected that the Harper government would assert federal paramountcy. Actions could have been taken in 2014 and early 2015, but inaction then resulted in a missed opportunity by early 2017 — a very costly missed opportunity, considering Northern Gateway's scale, timing advantage, and geography, and the market diversity it would have offered.

In 2011 the advent of LNG development in the Kitimat area gave proximate coastal First Nations a separate option for significant benefit based on natural gas rather than Alberta bitumen — an option with which they were much more amenable.

A sad postscript to the demise of Northern Gateway was the reaction from those First Nations along its pipeline route that had aligned themselves with the project — devastation and disappointment in the economic loss and the missed potential for genuine transformation of their communities. It is a sad reality, so at odds with the narrative within Canada of Indigenous opposition to resource development.

PETRONAS PACIFIC NORTHWEST LNG AND THE SHELL CONSORTIUM'S LNG CANADA

In late 2016, as the Trudeau government made its decisions on oil sands–related pipeline proposals, it also had to determine the fate of the project known as Pacific NorthWest LNG. In 2012 the Malaysian national oil company Petronas had made an audacious acquisition of northeast B.C. shale gas reserves developed by Progress Energy, a midsized Canadian producer, for approximately $6 billion in Canadian dollars. Petronas proposed to ship the gas by pipeline to Prince Rupert, convert it to liquefied natural gas, and export the product in tankers to Asian markets.

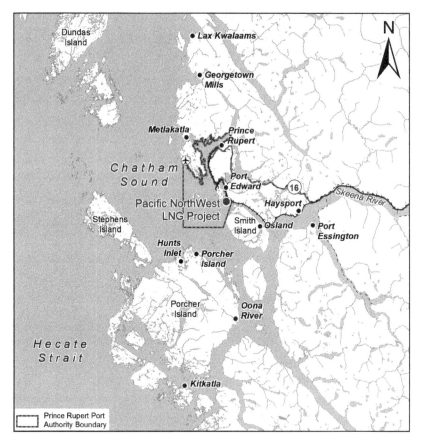

Source: Stantec
LNG Canada Site

LNG is created by cooling natural gas sufficiently to change it to liquid phase, thereby reducing its volume to one six-hundredth of the original volume. The liquid is odourless, colourless, nontoxic, and noncorrosive. LNG is economic in circumstances where large gas reserves cannot reach certain major consumption areas by pipeline; in such cases, it is transported in specially designed cryogenic tankers. When LNG reaches its market, it is regasified and distributed in conventional gas distribution pipelines.

Global natural gas demand is projected to increase on the order of 1.5 percent per annum to 2040, largely in the form of LNG consumed in Asia and Western Europe. Various LNG suppliers around the world will continue to compete to meet that demand. Shipping natural gas as LNG is costlier than pipeline transport due to the liquefaction and regasification processes, but significant global gas reserves have no other option to access markets. Due to the advent of fracking technology, North America now has access to gas reserves formerly considered unrecoverable, more than sufficient to comprise the foundation of new LNG export capacity.[2]

The economics of converting North American natural gas to LNG for export is much more complex than in other locations. A developer in, say, Mozambique, East Timor, or Sakhalin Island, with a world-scale gas resource, has no market option but to convert to LNG and compete for market share based on respective competitive advantages. The resource has no other value. However, any gas resource in North America can be sold into the continental market, which creates a market value or opportunity cost that has to be taken into account when evaluating the relative costs of one potential LNG supply against another.

In 2010 and 2011, LNG prices were strong globally, while the advent of North American shale gas depressed North American gas prices. That lessened the competitive disadvantages of North American gas and allowed enough economic margin to justify diversifying the LNG supply portfolio to include North American production locations. Canada was deemed to have the competitive advantage of a regulatory and political system deemed reasonably efficient, predictable, grounded in the rule of law, and free of corruption, unlike some of the world's potential production locations.

These conditions led to the development of various Canadian LNG production projects, with the Petronas project among the most credible. Essentially, Canadian production locations could compete with comparable greenfield — meaning entirely new — U.S. Gulf Coast locations on the basis of relative gas costs and transit times to Asian markets in northern latitudes. By the end of 2012, Petronas rationalized proceeding with a world-scale project based on western Canadian gas, with a liquefaction facility in Prince Rupert, British Columbia. The total project investment was on the order of $11 billion in Canadian dollars. In the same time frame, Shell and its Asian partners announced a similar world-scale development, utilizing the Kitimat port. Initial expectations around these projects were high. It was expected that final investment decisions would be made as early as 2014, and that on-stream dates of 2018 could be achieved. The projects were, admittedly, ambitious, particularly considering that they would compete with various U.S. Gulf Coast brownfields — projects that convert regasification sites to liquefaction sites. But regardless of Canada's competitive challenges, two world-class players were committed to Canadian LNG development.

In terms of carbon-related resistance, the proponents hoped these projects could avoid the special opprobrium directed at the Canadian oil sands. LNG export to Asia, especially China, helps these countries substitute natural gas for coal in electric generation, leading to a reduction in emissions — though that reduction is offset to some extent by emissions generated in the liquefaction process, which requires burning natural gas. Other incremental emissions arise from the natural gas production and transmission steps, due to the leakage of some methane.

Still, despite the contentions of various ENGOs to the contrary, a net carbon emissions reduction has been consistently attributed to these projects on a global basis, taking into account the full life cycle of the project. But, inescapably, any carbon emissions reduction would occur in Asia, not in Canada. That reality would remain an issue for those obsessed with Canada meeting its Paris commitment, or even with British Columbia meeting its self-imposed emissions reduction target. Despite the predictable resistance of Canadian ENGOs to these projects, however, the Canadian and B.C. governments recognized the global carbon emissions reduction benefit offered by the Petronas and Shell projects.

Both projects had contracted with TransCanada to build gas transmission trunk lines from the northeast B.C. extremity of its existing gas gathering system, known as NGTL, to their respective ports of Kitimat and Prince Rupert. Regulatory approvals for most of the additional facilities related to the Shell project were obtained by provincial regulatory authorities, not directly by federal environmental assessment agencies. Petronas found itself in a different circumstance altogether. Its liquefaction facility was planned for Lelu Island, just south of the Prince Rupert townsite, in the estuary of the Skeena River. Nearby Ridley Island was an alternative site for liquefaction facilities, but was held by other developers, not Petronas.

Lelu Island is Crown land, which meant the project could not use the provincial regulatory authorities via substitution provisions of the

Canadian Environmental Assessment Act (CEAA), as the Shell project had been able to do. Petronas was encouraged by both provincial and federal officials to use Lelu Island. At the outset of the fundamental design for the project, Petronas did not identify any biodiversity "showstoppers." Connecting the actual LNG supply to the tankers would require the construction of a trestle, essentially a bridge with LNG pipes along the top, going out into Prince Edward Sound, to depths where tankers could dock. This design would require supporting frames embedded into the seabed, including the area directly proximate to Lelu Island, known as Flora Bank, a sandy eelgrass bed that provides an important habitat for juvenile salmon. Initial filings by the project proponents with the Canadian Environmental Assessment Agency (CEAA) indicated that Petronas's environmental assessment team believed the trestle's construction and long-term installation would not materially impact salmon stocks in the area.[3]

Petronas delivered in its first environmental filings in February 2014. The initial design included a fairly conventional trestle design: a 3 kilometre trestle between the liquefaction facility and the docking station, supported by pylons in the Flora Bank eelgrass mudflat. However, because of concerns from various relevant stakeholders, most notably local First Nations, that installing the trestle supports within Flora Bank would unduly impact juvenile salmon, Petronas filed a supplementary document with the CEAA in October 2014, with a new trestle design that included a 1.6 kilometre suspension bridge over Flora Bank. This suspension bridge would connect with a conventional 1.1 kilometre trestle heading out to docking locations in Chatham Sound. This audacious design was akin to building the Golden Gate Bridge and connecting it with a massive cement block installed at depths of more than one thousand feet.[4]

Even as the project's environmental assessment carried on throughout 2015, Petronas announced midyear that it would make no final investment decision until it had an approval from the B.C. legislature and had cleared the federal environmental assessment review process. Petronas persevered with the project despite a collapse in global LNG pricing in 2014 and 2015, which was largely driven by a similar collapse in global crude oil prices. It would receive no final decision from the Harper or Trudeau governments on the project for roughly another eighteen months. That decision would depend on an assessment of possible salmon impacts at Flora Bank and rationalizing incremental carbon emissions.

In February 2016, the CEAA released a draft report concluding that the project was "not likely to cause significant adverse environmental effects taking into account the implementation of the key mitigation measures." (The agency had started its review of Pacific NorthWest LNG in April 2013.) Now a new thirty-day public comment period would begin. In the normal course of things, that period would end mid-March, and the government would announce its final decision by the end of March 2016. But within weeks of the draft report's release, McKenna acceded to pressure from various ENGOs and First Nations that objected to the draft report's basic conclusion, and she agreed to a three-month extension. These groups contended that federal officials had relied too much on analysis supplied by the applicant. The CEAA requested supplemental information from Petronas over the spring and summer of 2016. Petronas's hopes to make a final investment decision in mid-2016 were scuttled.

Finally, on September 27, 2016, McKenna announced that the project was approved, albeit with 190 conditions.[5] Within days, ENGO entities and certain coastal First Nations near Prince Rupert vowed litigation to overturn this conditional approval, based on the entirely predictable contention of inadequate consultation. Petronas responded cautiously to the approval, citing that it needed some months to assess whether it could comply with all 190 conditions, which included reducing the proposed attributable emissions to levels comparable with LNG Canada's commitments.

Apart from concerns on salmon, many within the Canadian environmentalist movement contended that Petronas's project would destroy any chance of British Columbia meeting its carbon emissions reduction targets. Nevertheless, support remained intact from the two major provincial parties — the incumbent Liberals led by Premier Christy Clark and the NDP opposition. Petronas assessed "cost optimization" options through the first quarter of 2017 — at least, that was its public position. It offered no specific date for a final investment decision. Meanwhile, British Gas had been acquired by Shell Oil and was no longer committed to a liquefaction facility on Ridley Island. That meant Petronas could relocate from Lelu, avoiding Flora Bank and obviating the need for a suspension bridge. This relocation option was a fundamentally sound change to the project, and Petronas remained in talks with the federal government over the first half of 2017, exploring what kind of supplemental environmental review a relocation would require.

In light of 2017 LNG prices, and of short-term supply and demand balances, conflicting views prevailed on the fundamental competitiveness of LNG production from Canada. However, experts predicted a second wave of required LNG liquefaction facilities after 2020, which would accommodate the Canadian options caught up for much of the decade in protracted regulatory approvals. For Petronas, the questions around relocating Pacific NorthWest LNG's liquefaction facility and fundamental LNG market considerations remained in play over the first half of 2017, notwithstanding existing litigation risk and no facilitating accommodations from the federal government. Regrettably, in mid-July, another setback occurred.

The Federal Court of Appeal ruled that the NEB must reconsider whether the natural gas trunk line into Prince Rupert to be built by TransCanada fell within provincial or federal jurisdiction, thereby nullifying the existing provincial approvals. The project now faced another, redundant regulatory step, even if it could find its way to Ridley Island.

Sadly, on July 25, 2017, the project was terminated. Petronas attributed the decision to an "extremely challenging environment." To that point, Pacific NorthWest had spent $400 million on advancing the project through provincial and federal regulatory processes. Petronas had bought Progress Energy for $6 billion in 2012, and at one point had spent $2 billion a year to prove up the subsidiary's natural gas reserves. Canadian energy commentators debated the cause of this termination: How much was attributable to market conditions and the inferior competitive position of Canada as an LNG location, and how much could be attributed to a protracted regulatory process, typified by equivocation and revision, that piled uncertainty and cost on Petronas for close to four years? Was so much time really required to determine whether salmon impacts constituted a real showstopper? Whatever the reasons, the reality was that Canada lost a project that would have represented real value, especially for the country's struggling natural gas production sector, and improved the world's emissions position.

ENERGY EAST

Energy East was conceived in November 2011, within weeks of Obama demanding KXL's reroute, which was that project's first major setback and the first strong sign that a permit might never be forthcoming under the Obama administration. With Energy East, TransCanada proposed to take Alberta's diluted bitumen east to refineries and export terminals in Quebec and potentially to the Maritimes. Public disclosure of TransCanada's intention to move forward with the project did not occur until August 2013, after it had obtained substantial commercial support along with other important alignments with key stakeholders in the gas distribution sector. The project's scale of 900,000 barrels per day rivalled KXL's 1.1 million barrels per day, and it had binding long-term contracts with producers and refiners. The project was expected to cost approximately $12 billion for its new-build elements, with an in-service date of late 2017 for deliveries to Quebec and 2018 for deliveries to New Brunswick.

Predictably, the Harper government was a strong advocate of the project from the outset, identifying fully with its unique attributes of providing tidewater access while bringing Canadian crude to national markets currently supplied by foreign oil. What project could have more "pan-Canadian" elements? Ontario's and Quebec's leaders reacted, at least at first, with no hostility. New Brunswick politicians were unequivocally supportive, embracing the investment and related employment benefits. As for Trudeau and Mulcair, their positions were

Source: TransCanada; The Canadian Press
Energy East Route

fundamentally equivocal. Neither outright opposed the project. Both conceded that the project had some positive attributes, particularly in terms of national security of supply, economic impact, and market access, although they declared that their positions were contingent on the results of the regulatory process. But Mulcair, a long-time Quebec politician and former environment minister, repeatedly referred to deficiencies in the regulatory process, especially in respect of how it dealt with climate impacts. And Trudeau vacillated depending on his audience. On some occasions he would invoke a nebulous social licence standard as necessary for the project's approval, and then on others he would acknowledge the project's significant economic impact for New Brunswick and Alberta production interests.

Quebec had concerns related to the project based on spill risk, carbon impacts, and First Nations issues. But also in play was a venality akin to that shown by Christy Clark in respect of oil pipeline infrastructure on the West Coast — too much economic value, other provincial governments felt, would accrue to Alberta and hydrocarbon producers, and not enough to the provinces bearing the additional risks of the bitumen in the pipeline, notwithstanding how material or mitigatable those risks may be. As long as the Energy East regulatory process remained open, neither Trudeau or Mulcair had to take a definitive position, regardless of the project's obvious benefits for Canada.

The cost of Energy East's long haul east — from Alberta to New Brunswick — was mitigated by the fact that TransCanada owned an underutilized gas line all the way from Alberta to North Bay, Ontario. It planned to convert that pipe, and to build new pipe only from North Bay through Quebec and into New Brunswick, terminating at the existing refinery in Saint John. Shipping costs, given the scale of the project, could approximate the levels achieved on KXL to the U.S. Gulf Coast. TransCanada achieved contractual support for Energy East for the majority of its 800,000 barrel capacity, this despite the fact that Alberta oil sands producers had already collectively committed to four other pipeline projects. If all these projects were built, pipeline capacity would exceed most estimates for crude oil production achievable by the next decade. As of mid-2013 all five projects were still in play, their respective proponents working diligently for approval; nevertheless, the producers clearly saw value in maintaining market access options.

The original design had the Energy East terminus in a town called Gros Cacouna, in upper Gaspé, Quebec, near the mouth of the St. Lawrence. The Quebec terminal offered shippers a shorter haul than a New Brunswick terminal would, and Gros Cacouna was a world-class port, with the access and depth that the tankers for this project would require. The terminal would also provide additional capital spending within Quebec, with the attendant employment benefits, both in construction and operations.

The project, from its initial disclosure, faced resistance from the gas distribution companies of Ontario and Quebec over the existing gas pipe that would be converted to crude oil service. West of North Bay, Ontario, there was no issue, but the section between North Bay and Ottawa was more contentious. That section was occasionally required to meet peak-day gas demand in Ontario and Quebec through the winter heating season. TransCanada eventually resolved the situation by acquiescing to the distributors' demands, agreeing to provide additional infrastructure closer to North Bay and providing other accommodations to maintain peak-day capacity. This added cost to the project from the perspective of the prospective shippers and TransCanada, but it did resolve a major irritant that could have diminished net benefits to both Ontario and Quebec. It is worth noting that the owners of those distribution companies, Enbridge and Spectra, were two of TransCanada's most direct commercial competitors. Achieving consensus with them on the collateral gas impacts from Energy East was a significant achievement.

The Harper government remained unequivocally supportive of Energy East, even as the regulatory process still had to be completed. In many ways, Harper's attitude was the inverse of Trudeau's and Mulcair's; the regulatory process would ultimately affirm projects that offered substantial economic value to Canada and with no obvious showstopper environmental impacts, including carbon emissions. For Trudeau and Mulcair, the regulatory process offered the possibility that rejection would provide a way out of imposing a project of national benefit on Quebec. The Couillard government in Quebec City had yet to decide if it could even abide by this project, let alone decide what price it would demand.

Ultimately, Trudeau and Mulcair should have expected the NEB process to replicate the same outcome rendered for Northern Gateway, especially if the issue of attributable carbon emissions was considered out of scope. If carbon considerations were to nullify Energy East, the government of the day should have clarified the issue as a matter of policy, not delegated it to the regulators. Of course, that scoping decision excluding carbon emissions only embittered Canadian ENGOs. Energy East consisted substantially of converted existing pipe, with its new build over relatively benign terrain, including a St. Lawrence River crossing. The NEB would approve this project if its disposition toward Northern Gateway and TMX provided any guidance. TransCanada and its customers clearly expected approval, as evidenced by the hundreds of millions of dollars they spent on filing, stakeholder consultation, and public advocacy, relying on the past record of the NEB.

Quebec had endured the Lac-Mégantic incident in June 2013, when an unattended seventy-four-car freight train carrying Bakken Formation crude oil rolled down a 1.2 percent grade and derailed. The train caught fire, and multiple tank cars exploded. Forty-two people were confirmed dead, with five more missing and presumed dead. This incident should have underscored the superior safety and spill risk attributes of pipelines relative to rail transport; instead, the Quebec political class simply believed that any mid-continent crude oil moving through the province, substantially for export, posed an unacceptable additional risk. Ontario and Quebec remained officially equivocal about Energy East through 2015.

At the end of 2015, almost eighteen months after TransCanada made its initial filings for the project in its original configuration, it announced that in response to two-plus years of consultation and stakeholder feedback it would change the pipeline's route in various ways, and would delete the Quebec oil terminal at Gros Cacouna. According to the original estimate, the project would cost $12 billion, but TransCanada revised that to $15.7 billion, not counting the value of existing pipeline assets that would be converted. Admittedly, TransCanada might have better anticipated the deficiencies of the Gros Cacouna terminal site, specifically the impacts on beluga populations in the Gulf of St. Lawrence. In any event, TransCanada still expected to start construction in 2018 and to have the pipeline in service in 2020.

Incredibly, before the NEB determined that TransCanada had submitted a complete application — a necessary condition for the hearing phase of the regulatory process to begin — it informed TransCanada that its revised application was too complex and needed to be "simplified." This unprecedented action by the NEB served to stretch out the timeline, and brought greater cost that the project would have to bear.

Why did TransCanada persevere with Energy East until the end of 2015, despite the revisions, cost escalations, and an increasingly negative reaction from Quebec? The answer is that two other major options for market access had been lost. Obama had rejected KXL in mid-November, while Trudeau's election in October and the subsequent tanker ban signalled dim prospects for Northern Gateway. As large-scale options, only Energy East and TMX remained. Energy East at that point seemed validated as another all-Canadian market access option.

As a project that traversed most of the country, carrying crude oil intended mostly for export, Energy East obviously fell under federal jurisdiction. TransCanada had, therefore, always relied on the project being regulated federally. Regardless of that legal reality, however, the Quebec provincial government insisted that the project submit itself to a provincial environmental assessment process. Implausibly, Quebec claimed this demand signalled no intention to block the pipeline, claiming that it was merely necessary in order for TransCanada to follow provincial law. But to what end, for a project under federal jurisdiction? Did opponents of the project believe a Quebec environmental assessment process might be more stringent, with broader scope, and prove less sympathetic to the proponents than the NEB had? Was it a demand for a veto on the project?

Equally implausibly, both Trudeau and Notley were pliant, preferring to placate Quebec sensitivities, which they rationalized with vague invocations of improved social licence. Neither took a stand for the federal paramountcy on jurisdiction, nor did they show any regard for the cost and ambiguity they created by acceding to Quebec's demand. After all, Quebec threatened to seek an injunction to halt the project until TransCanada acceded.

Sadly, in April 2016 TransCanada did just that, agreeing to carry out a parallel Quebec assessment. In return, the Quebec government promised that by 2018 it would provide a definitive position on Energy East — as if that were a necessary condition for the project to proceed.

This episode, along with other demonstrations of opposition from Quebec politicians, especially the mayor of Montreal, Denis Coderre, only increased the regional tensions in play. Having the tanker terminal only in New Brunswick reduced environmental risks for Quebec, but the real issue pertained to relative risk-reward, given that the project's major economic returns would accrue to Alberta and private sector interests, not Quebec. TransCanada had planned Energy East with the understanding that a traditional NEB regulatory process would ensue, and that any federal government would defer to an NEB recommendation, and not de facto extend vetoes to certain provinces. The reality was that the project would provide significant net economic benefits to Quebec and Ontario, primarily in the form of construction spending, property tax contribution, and additional employment in operations, without any special accommodations from Alberta or the Energy East shippers.

Almost six months passed before the NEB was prepared to make a determination of completeness of the Energy East application, and only with such a determination in place would the NEB begin the twenty-four-month

Protestors disrupt Energy East National Energy Board hearing, Montreal, August 2016.

process to generate a final recommendation. TransCanada would not achieve regulatory approval until late 2018 at the earliest. Hearings for Energy East were to commence, finally, in Montreal, on August 29, 2016. But the hearings were cancelled, even before they formally began, when protesters stormed the room. The second day of hearings was postponed, but no new date was given. It is hard to understand how the NEB failed to coordinate adequate security procedures with local or federal policing authorities to ensure normal decorum. A fiasco.

Even worse for the NEB, two of the board's panel members tasked with carrying out the Energy East regulatory process had, as a news report revealed, met with ex-Quebec premier Jean Charest while he was a paid consultant for TransCanada. The NEB was confronted with motions to stop proceedings, remove the existing panel entirely, and restart proceedings with new, untainted panel members.

The two panel members whose impartiality was cast into doubt were Lyne Mercier and Jacques Gauthier. The Trudeau government had encouraged an NEB initiative to engage with Canadians to clarify the board's functions and accountabilities, in the hope of improving "trust and confidence." Along with NEB chairman Peter Watson, Mercier and Gauthier had met with former Quebec premier Jean Charest as part of that initiative to solicit his views on how the NEB could better engage with Quebecers. Watson clarified at the meeting's outset that direct discussion of Energy East was out of bounds, and notes from the meeting attest that the topic did not arise. The NEB participants did not know TransCanada had contracted Charest as a lobbyist to provide them with strategic advice on progressing the Energy East project within Quebec, and they contended that they were not lobbied in any way during the meeting. The Energy East project was not discussed, including procedural issues related to it. None of those facts were enough to keep the panel in place. In the first week of September 2016, the NEB stated that "all three panel members have decided to recuse themselves in order to preserve the integrity of the National Energy Board and of the Energy East and Eastern Mainline Review. The members acted in good faith."

The ENGO opposition welcomed this development. At the very least it would stretch out the regulatory process. Months, perhaps even a year, would be consumed with installing a new panel and planning the hearings again. Not until December were three new panel members appointed, none of whom had previous NEB experience or comparable regulatory experience.

All three were from Quebec or New Brunswick. Of course, as this unfolded, Trump was elected. KXL was back in play. How that would impact TransCanada's resolve to persevere remained to be seen. However, Energy East's contractual support remained in place into 2017.

Just a few weeks after their formal installation, the new NEB panel members decided to throw out all decisions made by the previous panel. The board said all hearing steps and related deadlines for the TransCanada project no longer applied. That included the determination that the Energy East application was "complete," rulings on participation, the hearing order, and the issues list. Any hope of a decision by 2018 was now undone. Why? Ostensibly, the new panel wished to remove completely any taint from the prior process, but it showed no transparent rationale to justify the costs that would arise from further delay.

A final straw broke the camel's back. On August 23, 2017, in a decision avidly supported by the project's opponents, especially the ENGOs, the new panel announced that it would consider attributable upstream and downstream greenhouse gas emission issues related to Energy East. This decision contradicted an agreement made in December 2016 between the Government of Canada, via Environment Canada, and the NEB, that the assessment of attributable carbon effects from Energy East would be outside the scope of the NEB regulatory process, and would be dealt with as it had been with TMX and Northern Gateway.[6] That agreement would have left Environment Canada and, implicitly, the federal Cabinet, to judge whether any determined attributable incremental emissions were material enough to invalidate the project. They would have assessed the trade-off between meeting carbon reduction targets and seizing economic value. That agreement was set aside by the new panel, and with no apparent opposition from the Trudeau government. Throughout 2017, the Trudeau government never intervened in the actions of this new panel, showing its tacit approval. In early September TransCanada suspended all project activity for thirty days, citing "significant changes" in the regulatory process. The suspension doubtlessly allowed the Trudeau government time to reconsider intervening in the NEB panel's course. Predictably, Alberta's and New Brunswick's premiers issued pleas to salvage the project.

A month later, on October 5, TransCanada announced the termination of the project, citing, somewhat euphemistically, a "careful review of changed circumstances." It also disclosed a $1 billion writeoff of expenses incurred to date. Montreal Mayor Coderre claimed an "outstanding victory," continuing to condemn TransCanada for its "arrogance and condescension." Similar invocations of victory came from the expected entities that had consistently opposed the project.

More significant was the tepid response from federal energy minister Carr, who rationalized the termination as a business decision of TransCanada's, driven principally by changed commodity prices.[7] His remarks included no concession that the federal regulatory process had contributed to costs and delays, nor that the federal government could have fought much harder for its own jurisdiction to determine the project's merits with a national benefits test. Carr certainly did not concede that the federal government had only added to the whole process's uncertainty and dysfunction. Notley was disappointed, but she did not attribute any blame to the federal regulatory process, nor to the Trudeau government specifically. Trudeau objected when the political opposition criticized him over Energy East's termination, accusing them of "stoking national divisions." Again, he accepted no culpability, and neither did he acknowledge that losing this market access option was a serious issue.

Commentators debated to what extent the decision to terminate had been driven by KXL's revival and the TMX and Line 3 approvals, all of which obviated the need for Energy East.[8] For TransCanada, terminating Energy East would only facilitate re-contracting KXL. Others emphasized that TransCanada and its shippers may have persevered if only the regulatory process had not been so perverse, with its amendments, recusal, rescoping, and refusal by the federal government to insist on the paramountcy of its jurisdiction in the matter. An approval could have been well worthwhile, even if construction were deferred to the late 2020s when market conditions justified it. If the Trudeau government had seen value in the project in the long term, how could it have allowed the protracted regulatory processes to have been imposed on it? And how could it not have defended the project against unfair claims from elements within Quebec? Was it simply incapable of ever asserting federal authority on Quebec for a project without overwhelming public support within the province, regardless of national benefit? Did Trudeau prefer a seemingly endless regulatory process as a preferable default? If so, he acted without regard for Canada's credibility as a jurisdiction for investment of private capital for major infrastructure projects.

The facts of 2017's three lost projects speak for themselves. Apparent approvals undone after the fact, fundamental scoping decisions revisited well after incurral of major financial expenditures, protracted hearings generating little probative value, and excessive delay in federal decision-making, with a federal government seemingly indifferent to how capital is forced to react to the government's dysfunction. The loss of three significant projects made even more crucial the necessity of realizing the remaining pipeline alternatives.

Although the essential understanding between Notley and Trudeau remained intact, arguably reinforced by the surprise revival of KXL, in all three cases the Trudeau government revealed a fundamental equivocation on the merits of hydrocarbon expansion. Its disposition toward the projects lost in 2016 and 2017 demonstrated its skepticism of existing regulatory processes, considering them too supportive of hydrocarbon infrastructure approvals. The genuine convictions of the Trudeau government would be tested, ultimately, with TMX. Could the project get to construction? If not, Trudeau and his government would inescapably face a real breakdown with Notley and Alberta.

But 2017 also saw the Liberals' other great initiative unfold. They set out to change the NEB regulatory process, the process that continued to generate approvals and alienate environmentalists. Trudeau's government set out to devise a new system so rigorous, so sympathetic to ENGOs, First Nations, and the political left, that only the least contentious projects would pass muster. Approvals of such projects, if they even existed in the real world, would leave little political issue for any federal government to deal with.

But more likely, the new system under Bill C-69 would prove a poison pill to future hydrocarbon infrastructure development.

CHAPTER 4

Bill C-69: Poison Pill

A MONTH AFTER he was elected prime minister in 2006, Stephen Harper was in London for a G8 meeting, and he made his famous speech to an audience of Canadian and British business leaders, proclaiming Canada an emerging "global energy superpower."[1] The price of crude oil had tripled since the 1990s, and the Canadian oil sands resource was "in the money" as a significant component of world crude oil supply. Similarly, continental natural gas prices were at historical highs, potentially sufficient even to validate developing remote gas sites such as the Mackenzie Delta. Harper went on to extol Canada's world-class regulatory system and long-standing record of national commitment to security and rule of law compared with most of the world's crude oil supply sources.

Harper's observations were entirely logical. The scope of potential development would reach over $500 billion by the middle of the next decade.[2] He described his vision without even trying to rationalize it to a world seemingly committed to dealing collectively with the climate change risk. Neither did he acknowledge that Canadian oil sands, in terms of emissions generated per unit of output, represent one of the most carbon intensive sources of crude oil in the world. He went on to withdraw Canada from the Kyoto protocol in 2012, to reduce spending on various existing "green initiatives," and, as always, to eschew carbon pricing via a transparent national carbon tax as Canada's pre-eminent carbon policy instrument.

Harper's fundamental position on hydrocarbon development was entirely aligned with the position held by Alberta's various Progressive Conservative governments, all of which had presided over the massive investment buildup in the oil sands from 2000 to 2014. The province was responsible for administering environmental assessments for upstream investment within its borders, and that process remained pliant, notwithstanding ENGO concerns about cumulative effects of unconstrained oil sands development. Given Alberta's long-standing conservative political culture and the positive economic conditions arising from hydrocarbon investment and strong commodity pricing, the ENGOs were unlikely to achieve any policy breakthrough via the electoral process. Moreover, the Harper Conservatives were building to their 2011 majority. ENGO frustration peaked as the 2000s evolved with ever greater buildup in oil sands production capacity. In response, the ENGOs assaulted infrastructure through the regulatory process as an alternative to a policy breakthrough.

In 2008, at a meeting sponsored by the Rockefeller Brothers Fund, American and Canadian ENGOs committed themselves to using all the regulatory obstruction and related litigation they could muster to stop pipelines that would provide market access for expanding oil sands production. Of course, a similar dynamic played out with KXL on the U.S. side, and with Northern Gateway in Canada. To assist them in their battles, Canadian ENGOs received funding from U.S. entities such as the Pew Charitable Trust, the Rockefeller Foundation, and the Hewlett Trust on the order of hundreds of millions of dollars.[3]

As a measure of the evolving polarization, federal energy minister Joe Oliver wrote an open letter in early 2012 just before the start of the Northern Gateway hearings and just after Obama's first intervention to frustrate the KXL pipeline in late November 2011. Referring to ENGOs and those that fund them, he wrote:

> These groups threaten to hijack our regulatory system
> to achieve their radical ideological agenda. They seek
> to exploit any loophole they can find, stacking public

hearings with bodies to ensure that delays kill good projects. They use funding from foreign special interest groups to undermine Canada's national economic interest.... They do this because they know it can work. It works because it helps them to achieve their ultimate objective: delay a project to the point it becomes economically unviable.... In many cases, these projects would create thousands upon thousands of jobs for Canadians, yet they can take years to get started due to the slow, complex and cumbersome federal government approval process.[4]

Naturally, Canadian ENGOs resented Oliver calling them "radicals"; in their view, no cause was more valid or morally compelling than avoiding global climate change or protecting unique Canadian geography from potential oil spills and other physical disruption. But their arguments did not acknowledge the economic cost to Canada of failing to realize its hydrocarbon potential; they offered, instead, only vague invocations of a transition to a "greener economy."[5] They would never discuss climate change risk as a cost and benefit issue. They saw only a moral imperative. Of course, climate change is a real risk, and Oliver's rhetoric was unhelpful, making it more difficult for Canadians to reach a consensus on the optimal mix of carbon policies to avoid catastrophic risk at reasonable economic cost, both nationally and globally.

The Harper government responded to environmentalist pressures by incorporating in its Bill C-38, an omnibus budget bill, specific adjustments to the existing federal regulatory approval process for major projects and amendments to the Canadian Environmental Assessment Act. The changes were enacted in 2012, too late for Northern Gateway, but in time to be applied to TMX. Northern Gateway's experience highlighted the capacity of the ENGOs to mobilize resistance, stretch out the hearing process, and dominate much of the media coverage to their advantage — their later victory in having the pipeline cancelled would validate their tactics.

The specific amendments Harper achieved with Bill C-38 were four-fold.[6] First, Cabinet, not the regulator, would make the final decision on any given project. Cabinet would receive recommendations based on the regulatory process, but it would have the discretion to accept or reject any such recommendations, and also the power to impose an approval. Second, a deadline would be imposed on the regulatory review of the project — going forward, it was mandated that a review must be completed fifteen months after an application is deemed complete. Third, standing — the right to present evidence and make closing arguments at regulatory proceedings — would be restricted to individuals directly impacted by the proposed project and those who provide some probative value to proceedings. The fourth amendment concerned scope: review would be restricted to impacts that result directly from the proposed project, specifically excluding upstream and downstream carbon emissions. For Canadian ENGOs, this created a "dark shadow over NEB proceedings."[7] They bitterly resented how Harper's mandatory timelines and standing provisions would guide the regulatory process for TMX. Somewhat ironically, Cabinet's final decision-making authority would devolve upon Justin Trudeau in 2016, allowing him explicit discretion to terminate Northern Gateway.

As constructive as these amendments were for regulatory efficiency and political accountability, the Harper government missed an opportunity for genuine reform of a core deficiency to reduce regulatory risk for proponents. Even with the C-38 amendments, determination that a project was in the public interest, which provided political sanction for the project, would still come at the end of the process, after the applicant had spent hundreds of millions of dollars. The applicant was still, therefore, unreasonably vulnerable to an ultimate "no" long after it had invested vast amounts of money. Traditionally, the question of whether extracting hydrocarbons was in the public interest had been a non-issue, but that was and is no longer the case, certainly not since Canada's participation in the UN climate process in 1992. Given that, a transparent, rational, and efficient process is necessary to determine whether or not an energy project is in the public interest. Canada needs a process that compels a political judgment as early as possible on the desirability of a project, in order to reduce risk to proponents so that they can justify the cost of the regulatory approval process itself. With that initial determination in hand, a second phase should establish specific conditions on construction and operations, and should proceed solely in the hands of the regulators, not the politicians.

On the balance, Bill C-38 amounted to tactical process improvements that, at the margin, would create a more efficient, more direct process, as long as the appointed regulators and politicians applied its provisions vigorously. Nevertheless, the amendments were deeply resented by the ENGO community and Canada's political left, as was any change that reduced the capacity for obstruction.

The Liberal platform document for the 2015 election clearly laid out that a Trudeau government would seek to redress Harper's CEAA 2012, the term that would come to describe the federal regulatory system created after passage of C-38. It never conceded, however, that doing so would enable the obstructionist agenda of the opponents of hydrocarbon development, and possibly to any major energy developments. Trudeau's audacious intent would be to make the federal regulatory system "credible again."[8] Any regulatory process that recommended Northern Gateway's approval — albeit a conditional approval — had no credibility. However, the Liberal platform document never cited any specific deficiencies in the regulatory conditions imposed on route, engineering, safety proceedings, emergency response, and other stakeholder concessions related to the NEB Northern Gateway approval. Instead, it invoked, however inchoately, the Great Bear Rainforest as needing total protection, incapable of facing any level of spill risk without consideration of the attendant economic value loss.

The Liberal platform document did not specifically equate "restoring public trust" with denying projects, but it certainly gave no credit to Canadian hydrocarbons for their economic contribution. It did not substantiate how the process preceding 2015 had failed to meet those standards. The Liberals intended to create a process so rigorous and so inclusive, and informed by such appropriate policy direction, that only low-carbon projects with sufficient social licence could pass muster, allowing a future Liberal government to approve them without feeling morally compromised. What real-world project within Canada of any materiality would self-evidently pass such muster? Keep thinking.

Within days of Trudeau's election, mandate letters were issued to the ministers of energy and environment. Consider the Carr mandate letter; it contained nothing about resolving market access as key priority, nor did it stress responding to competitiveness concerns of the Canadian hydrocarbon industry. What it did prioritize was the following:

> Work with the Minister of Environment and Climate Change, the Minister of Fisheries, Oceans and the Canadian Coast Guard, and the Minister of Indigenous and Northern Affairs to immediately review Canada's environmental assessment processes to regain public trust and introduce new, fair processes that will: restore robust oversight and thorough environmental assessments of areas under federal jurisdiction, while also working with provinces and territories to avoid duplication; ensure that decisions are based on science, facts, and evidence, and serve the public's interest; provide ways for Canadians to express their views and opportunities for experts to meaningfully participate, including provisions to enhance the engagement of Indigenous groups in reviewing and monitoring major resource development projects; and require project proponents to choose the best technologies available to reduce environmental impacts.[9]

Carr was to carry out this contribution to regulatory reform subordinate to the minister of the environment, Catherine McKenna. The McKenna mandate letter clearly placed her in the lead on the regulatory reform process, stating that she, "supported by the Ministers of Fisheries, Oceans and the Canadian Coast Guard, and Natural Resources," was to "immediately review Canada's environmental assessment processes to regain public trust."[10] This prioritization of accountabilities is consistent with a mindset that environmental assessment is a virtual end in itself, not a process to efficiently and competently validate alignment with the public interest and then establish appropriate conditions on projects' construction and operations, including certain stakeholder accommodation.

Furthermore, according to this vision, if environmental assessment was not to comprise outright obstruction of development, it would create a process so "robust" that any project it recommended would pass muster with even the most ardent of ENGOs. Could that ever include a hydrocarbon-based project? Hardly. But that was never clarified forthrightly by these ministers or the Trudeau government.

Carr was also specifically tasked to "modernize the National Energy Board, ensuring composition reflects regional views and has sufficient expertise in fields such as environmental science, community development, and Indigenous traditional knowledge." Not that those deficiencies had been substantiated — but again, why not deconstruct the regulatory process that had failed so obviously by approving Northern Gateway?

Throughout 2016, as the Trudeau government made its pipeline decisions and tried to achieve full buy-in from the provinces for federal climate policy as laid out in the Pan-Canadian Framework on Clean Growth and Climate Change, it also took the next steps on regulatory reform. It created two expert panels, one to deal with changes in the assessment process itself, the other to deal with NEB modernization.[11] The approach was curious, given that the NEB had jurisdiction over major energy project approvals. Changing the process of environmental assessment meant changing the NEB process, presumably to modernize it. The two panels were distinct in ways that would give rise to fundamentally different recommendations.

The modernization panel, which published its reports in the first half of 2017, had members whose professional resumés showed closer connection to the energy industry, specifically to the Canadian pipeline industry. It ultimately recommended a two-step regulatory process to secure a binding public interest determination early in the approval process.[12] This fundamental change responded to obvious deficiencies of the past ten years, whereby the regulatory process had become untenably risky. The modernization panel proposed that Cabinet must make its national interest determination for any proposed project within roughly one year, based on a strategic review, and this national interest determination would be performed "before the specific technical details of any project are even developed, but applying criteria such as net economic benefits, impact on and accommodation of Indigenous rights, significant or unique environmental effects, cumulative effects, and climate policy considerations."

Consultation with Indigenous entities would also have to be accommodated in this first phase. If a project achieved an affirmative determination, it would go on to a second phase: a detailed regulatory review and environmental assessment. But this second phase would not consider national interest or policy arguments already addressed in the first phase. This structure would restore the regulatory function to one of setting conditions on the construction and operations of proposed projects already deemed in the national interest. A political decision would come as early as possible in the process, not as late as possible.

The environmental assessment panel had, of course, an entirely distinct vision. This panel recommended fundamental changes in the decision model for project approval, essentially laying out a consensus-based approach with special emphasis on achieving Indigenous consent. As well, the basic criterion for approval would be a net benefit test based on what this panel viewed as the five pillars of sustainability: environmental, social, economic, health, and cultural well-being. The panel did not address the cost and time of its recommended process, other than to acknowledge that it would "cost more." It proposed that Cabinet hear appeals of the environmental assessment authority's decision only at the end of the process.

In the second half of 2017, the federal government issued a discussion paper that tried to synthesize the two panels' disparate recommendations and clearly indicate where it was headed in respect of regulatory reform. Most importantly, it rejected the major recommendation of the modernization panel. Cabinet would retain authority to make public interest determinations for designated projects subject to federal jurisdiction. The paper described how it envisioned the accountabilities for a new assessment agency, not the existing NEB and CEAA. A rebranded and diminished NEB would oversee operating infrastructure under federal jurisdiction. This assessment process would accept the broad sustainability criteria as set out by the environmental assessment panel, while avoiding the use of individual project reviews as a forum to discuss complex policy issues. Such policy discussions would instead take place in the context of "strategic assessments" and "regional assessments," which would inform project assessments. Proponents would be required to lead a new "early planning phase" to provide more clarity on the scope and scale of the assessment, and to inform the expected timeline for obtaining a decision. The discussion paper gave little guidance on timelines for completing assessments. As well, it provided no clarity on how assessment could proceed in a timely and cost-effective manner with no discretion to limit public involvement. The "standing test" currently incorporated into the National Energy Board Act was clearly under fire, such that inclusion was almost an end in itself — inclusion of any potential participant, regardless of the probative value of their evidence or whether they were directly impacted by the proposed project. Determination that a project was in the public interest would come at the end of the entire process, with no onus on the government of the day to convey as early as possible to proponents whether the possibility of an affirmative determination was fundamentally a non-starter.

Roughly six months later, in January 2018, the Trudeau government introduced Bill C-69. Its key provisions were not substantially different from what had been foreshadowed in the discussion paper that had preceded it.[13] In the House of Commons, the bill was reviewed only by the government majority–controlled Environment and Sustainable Development Committee — not the Natural Resources Committee; not Transport, Infrastructure and Communities; not International Trade; and not Finance — although those other committees and federal departments clearly had legitimate concerns about the impact of Bill C-69 on their areas of accountability.

Would it be an unreasonable conclusion to suggest that Bill C-69's basic provisions were designed to deter private sector entities from investing in energy infrastructure of any materiality, and perhaps even in hydrocarbon production itself? Was this bill architected as a poison pill, designed to inhibit the creation of future hydrocarbon infrastructure? An objective observer might answer "yes" to those questions. However, the government contended that the act's fundamental purpose was to foster "sustainability," defined as the ability to protect the environment; to contribute to the social and economic well-being of the people of Canada and preserve their health in a manner that benefits present and future generations; and to protect the environment and health, and social and economic conditions, insofar as they lie within Parliament's legislative authority.

Bill C-69 would create a new Impact Assessment Agency to lead the review of all major projects, assessing environmental, health, social, and economic impacts. The NEB was no longer accountable for such assessment within the overall approval process, and its other existing functions would be carried out by another new entity, the Canadian Energy Regulator. The CEAA's 2012 standing test was eliminated, such that public participation in the approval process was unconstrained, regardless of impacts on the overall efficiency of the process. The bill expanded the factors that must be assessed as bio-physical environmental effects, and also expanded the social, economic, and health effects that fall within Parliament's legislative jurisdiction, including a project's contribution to sustainability (as defined in the act).

According to C-69, Parliament must consider whether a project contributes to or hinders Canada's ability to meet its climate change commitments, must consider any adverse impact on the rights of the Indigenous Peoples of Canada recognized and affirmed by section 35 of the Constitution Act, 1982, and must consider the intersection of sex and gender, along with other identity factors. Parliament must also consider lower-impact alternatives to any given project. The impact assessment process now had three phases: a new planning phase, an assessment phase, and a decision-making phase. The timelines to complete any assessment remained at the discretion of the minister.

But the greatest failings of C-69 were those of omission. It put no onus on the federal government to state, within twelve months of a project's initial disclosure, where it stood with respect to the project in terms of its alignment with the public interest: a determination that should be a necessary condition before the project can proceed to a second phase to set specific conditions on operations and construction, including appropriate accommodation. C-69 placed no onus on the government to provide a rejection of a project as inconsistent with the public interest as soon as possible within that twelve-month period. Nor did it compel the government to identify specific potential "cumulative effects" — show-stoppers that a proponent should take under advisement. There was no absolute constraint on how long this pre-planning phase might run, but it had at least 180 days.

The second regulatory phase can impose significant conditions, even with an affirmative public interest determination already provided. As written, C-69 provided the federal government with maximum flexibility throughout the entire approval process. The government remained free to impose a political rejection based on policy and value considerations, even well after years and hundreds of millions of dollars had been expended. Furthermore, there was no onus on the government to clarify, as part of the assessment process, any "tipping points" related to specific cumulative effects. There was no onus to clarify how climate impacts would be evaluated for purposes of approval, and specifically whether any attributed emissions would automatically nullify a project.

The government did not attempt to clarify what constitutes adequate consultation and accommodation either as process or substance, nor to provide an objective standard consistent with current judicial rulings. Regulatory decisions on scoping — the boundaries of the assessment process, the project, and its direct impacts or something more open-ended — could still be revisited at any point in the process. C-69's rules might or might not be applicable to upstream hydrocarbon activity formerly handled exclusively by provincial regulation, such as natural gas fracking, and in situ tar sands production facilities. Key stages of the proposed impact assessment process remained subject to the considerable, some might say excessive, discretion enjoyed by various decision-makers in the new assessment process, most notably the minister of the environment. All of these deficiencies added risk onto private sector applicants, failing to provide clarity and fairness of process. Of course, capital would react to this. But perhaps that was the objective all along.

Admittedly, for Canadian industry to tolerate C-69, it would require significant amendment, even if its fundamental omissions were not to be

addressed. For instance, subjective social criteria such as gender considerations are beyond any reasonable scope for the assessment of a major
energy infrastructure project. The standing test, furthermore, had to be
restored. The regulatory approval process should be an efficiently managed technocratic exercise, not an open-ended focus group.

For the Canadian ENGO movement, Bill-C-69, as passed by the
House of Commons, was unequivocally a breakthrough. The assessment
process would now include a climate test, and that in itself was a real
barrier for any hydrocarbon-based project. The Pembina Institute stated:

> We were pleased to see important additions made to the
> Canadian Energy Regulator Act at the committee stage
> including the requirement to consider climate obligations
> in the review of all energy projects. In the twenty-first
> century, energy policy is climate policy and every deci-
> sion about energy infrastructure must be made with the
> end goal of achieving Canada's Paris Agreement commit-
> ments and decarbonization by mid-century. The gov-
> ernment now needs to initiate a robust strategic impact
> assessment of climate change to provide specific emis-
> sions thresholds and clear pathways to reach these goals.

Bill C-69 was formally introduced in early February of 2018, and the
House of Commons passed it with inconsequential amendments in June
of that year. However, the bill's progress through the Canadian Senate was
more problematic, as negative reaction to the legislation spread beyond
the hydrocarbon industry. Even the centrist *Globe and Mail* opined that
the legislation needed to be fundamentally reconsidered by the Trudeau
government. Nevertheless, the Trudeau government remained convinced
that its basic credibility rested on delivering C-69.

For most of 2017, however, voters with no direct connection to
the energy industry showed minimal concern with this bill. It was not
clear that Canadians outside of Alberta even knew that C-69 existed.
Certainly, in Alberta, C-69 soon became as much a source of alienation

and frustration as the lack of progress on market access. The Canadian ENGO movement, meanwhile, expected no less than C-69 from the Trudeau government, especially with its TMX approval and its acquiescence to the revived KXL.

But if C-69 was truly a poison pill for future hydrocarbon development in Canada, how could rationalizing any additional market access make sense? That remained the ENGOs' persistent question for the Trudeau government. Even if elements within the Trudeau government came to appreciate the visceral reaction to C-69 within significant elements of the Canadian hydrocarbon industry and other elements of the Canadian business community, the bill had to be delivered to the Canadian ENGO community. Otherwise, what environmentalist credibility would the Trudeau government retain?

As C-69 progressed through Parliament in 2018, Canadian public opinion grew increasingly polarized. By the fall of that year, the Notley government was fully engaged in asking for reconsideration of elements of C-69.[14] Notley was concerned, primarily, with how far C-69 would encroach on existing provincial environmental jurisdiction, especially in respect of upstream oil and gas activity. By October 2018 the Canadian hydrocarbon industry had called for the Trudeau government simply to stand down on the bill, despite how far its implementation had already evolved.[15] This added to the Canadian pipeline industry's long-standing opposition to the bill. At the end of 2018 C-69 was still being debated by the Canadian Senate; the Trudeau government gave no sign of reconsideration of its most contentious elements and omissions.

CHAPTER 5

Marching with Your Feet: TMX Bungled

DID THE TRUDEAU GOVERNMENT really find the Trans Mountain expansion project, with its terminus at Burnaby, more palatable than Northern Gateway, with its terminus at the Douglas Channel? In my view, probably not. It accepted the approval of TMX simply through a process of elimination.

Back in 2015, when Trudeau and Notley struck their quid pro quo, Energy East was deep in its regulatory process, and it was not clear that the Trudeau government would impose such a project on Quebec. Both Trudeau and Notley had acquiesced to Obama's denial of KXL and made no attempt to salvage it, and both were committed to denying Northern Gateway long before Trudeau became prime minister. Whether TMX was ideal no longer mattered. It was the only option left. Ultimately, the Trudeau government had to support some pipeline project to retain credibility, considering its avowed position on balance between the economy and the environment, let alone to ensure credible a carbon policy for Alberta.

Kinder Morgan is a legendary leading U.S. midstream energy-sector entity, highly esteemed within the industry for its commercial acumen in acquisition, corporate structuring, and low-cost operations. The company had acquired the existing Trans Mountain pipeline as part of a corporate acquisition of Terasen in 2005. It conceived the TMX expansion and established it commercially during the same 2011 to 2013 time frame in which TransCanada was progressing Energy East. The plan was to lay new pipe in the existing right of way, alongside the original Trans Mountain pipeline that had, since the 1950s, transported Alberta crude from Edmonton to Vancouver and Washington state refineries. Constructing TMX, at a cost originally estimated at $6.8 billion, would require debottlenecking existing pipe as well as building new pipe in certain sections outside of the existing right of way. The expansion would virtually triple the capacity of the pipeline, from 300,000 to 890,000 barrels per day. The project was a commercial response to the same fundamental supply and demand dynamics that had spawned KXL, Northern Gateway, and the rest. Growing Alberta diluted bitumen production would require substantial additional pipeline capacity over the decade from 2010 to 2020. TMX provided an alternative, with the fundamental advantage of using existing right of way and providing tidewater access for potential market diversity. By early 2013 sufficient shipper support was in hand from thirteen companies, representing 708,000 barrels per day of contracted commitments over fifteen to twenty years, to pay for the fundamental costs related to the transportation service of the pipeline. TMX's anticipated in-service date was late 2017.[1]

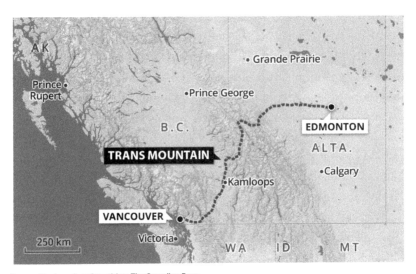

Source: Mapbox, OpenStreetMap; The Canadian Press
TMX Route

Kinder Morgan filed TMX's fifteen-thousand-page application with the NEB on December 17, 2013. In April 2014 the NEB clarified that it would render a decision by July 2015, so within fifteen months. The environmental assessment's scoping would exclude any issues related to upstream carbon impacts arising from oil sands development, along with downstream emissions arising from use of the transported oil. Participation in the TMX regulatory process was more constrained than it had been for Northern Gateway, both for those legitimately claiming direct impact and for those whose intervention came with information of probative value to the process. Out of over two thousand applicants for intervenor status, five hundred were denied. Even so, the NEB was hardly ruthless in how it applied its "direct impact" criterion. It handled most of the process with written interviews, and with some oral hearings related to traditional Indigenous knowledge.

Environmentalist groups staged public protests of TMX throughout 2014, most notably in response to tree clearing required to complete survey work necessary for the proponent's environmental assessment in the Burnaby area. Eventually, the B.C. Supreme Court provided an

Green Party leader Elizabeth May is arrested at a protest at the Trans Mountain facilities, March 2018.

injunction to remove protestors, and arrests followed. All of this added to the meme growing amongst Canadian ENGOs, that the NEB was a "captive regulator" to hydrocarbon proponents when it should be an "an impartial referee." They aimed most of this critique directly at the NEB's decisions to eschew traditional public hearings and to contain assessment scope to direct project impacts.

Partway through the regulatory process, TMX acceded to the demands of Burnaby-area stakeholders with a significant reroute around certain existing infrastructure. As a result, the approval process was extended for seven months, and the NEB recommended approval eventually in May 2016, albeit with 157 conditions. By statute, the Trudeau government would have seven months to decide on this recommendation.

Christy Clark, with her centre-right B.C. government, remained fundamentally equivocal about TMX, much as she had on Northern Gateway. She insisted that her five demands must be respected and met. Once again, Clark insisted that the project must come with

1. a successful environmental assessment;
2. commitment to a "world-class" marine spill response;
3. commitment to world-leading practices for land oil-spill prevention and response and recovery systems;
4. legal requirements met for Indigenous and treaty rights; and,
5. a fair share of fiscal and economic benefits for British Columbia, reflecting the level, degree, and nature of the risk borne by the province, the environment, and taxpayers.

This last demand was always the most problematic. How much financial compensation must the project, its shippers, and Alberta provide to British Columbia before a Clark government would approve the project?

The 2013 B.C. election had seen Clark's Liberals defeat the provincial NDP. Of course, voters cast their ballots for a variety of reasons, including the two parties' ideological differences, but it's fair to say that the election was largely determined by NDP leader Adrian Dix's decision, taken partway through the campaign, to oppose TMX outright. Dix's announcement led to a decisive positive turn in Liberal support. At least in 2013, British Columbians, expressing themselves through the electoral process, were not prepared to lose the project out of hand, despite the NDP's exhortations that TMX represented unconscionable risk in terms of both local spills and global climate impact. With Clark's re-election, the provincial government never actively resisted the project, but it expected additional financial compensation to resolve its alignment with the project. British Columbia did not object to the NEB process as it was applied, in rigid conformance to the regulatory changes that Harper's government had imposed in 2012, nor did it join any of the litigation directed at the project and the NEB.

One of the many ironies related to TMX was that no other major project developed over this era conformed so completely to the CEAA 2012 process — a process that would be replaced by Trudeau's C-69 initiative; yet the Trudeau government approved the project in late 2016, and went on to salvage it after Kinder Morgan decided to terminate it in 2018. Whatever the deficiencies the Trudeau government may have identified with the project's approval process under CEAA 2012, none justified denying or losing the project.

The Trudeau government did, however, undertake an assessment of climate impacts attributable to TMX, not as part of the NEB process but as a parallel exercise that would, at least officially, inform the government's ultimate approval of the project in late 2016. This assessment concluded that at its full scale, the project would create up to 26 MT of carbon-dioxide-equivalent upstream emissions per year. These emissions were not necessarily entirely incremental, the assessment conceded, and a series of contingencies would determine how many were incremental: the expected price of oil, the availability and costs of other transportation modes (for example, shipping crude by rail), and whether other pipeline projects were built.[2] The 26 MT figure was a maximum impact, assuming TMX carried only barrels that would not have been produced without its operation. This 26 MT per year was raised, of course, in the context of a Paris emissions reduction target on the order of 200 MT per year. This parallel process conceded that if oil sands production did not occur in Canada, other heavy-oil producers would capture that market share instead, such that global oil consumption would continue unabated in the absence of Canadian production growth.

The analysis also showed that in situ diluted bitumen from Alberta's oil sands had well-to-tank emissions in the same range as other types of heavy crude oil used in the Pacific market. The report concisely laid out the basic assumptions necessary to attribute incremental emissions to a major pipeline project based on the Canadian oil sands resource. Had the formal regulatory process dealt with determining attributable incremental emissions, would the outcome have been any better? Would a comparable analysis have to be repeated for every new oil sands project? Or could Canada internalize the fact that its diluted bitumen production had no impact on global heavy crude oil demand, and that it was therefore accountable for no material incremental global emissions?

Leading up to its November approval of TMX, the Trudeau government at no time offered an explicit rationalization of how the carbon impacts attributable to TMX would relate to national reduction targets, let alone what incremental emissions it attributed to the project. But even with all this ambiguity, Alberta's emissions cap of 100 MT was essential to ultimately rationalizing a TMX approval for the Trudeau government.

In May 2016 the NEB issued its report recommending approval of TMX, with 157 conditions. The Trudeau government had seven months to act on this recommendation. Virtually coincident with this release, the government announced a special review panel that would provide additional guidance on the ultimate disposition of TMX, also within the seven-month window. The panel's specific mandate was to complement the NEB review by identifying any gaps and issues of concern that the federal government should consider before deciding the pipeline's fate. The government was also obliged to carry out the last phase of consultation with affected First Nations, specifically in respect of the NEB recommendation to conditionally approve the project.

Within two months, the Federal Court of Appeal, in a non-unanimous decision, nullified Northern Gateway's approval. The Harper government had, the court ruled, failed to consult adequately with impacted First Nations during the same period now in play with TMX; that is, after the regulatory recommendation for approval and before the final Cabinet decision. The court set out, however ambiguously, a standard for more meaningful consultation. The Trudeau government, as I have discussed, could have remedied those deficiencies in respect of Northern Gateway, but chose not to. But now it was logical to presume that the government would apply the admonitions of the court in its current TMX consultation exercise over the summer and fall of 2016. For TMX, those two processes played out over the second half of 2016, while various groups long opposed to the project commenced litigation against the NEB process. Those claims were consolidated in early 2017 into a single proceeding before the Federal Court of Appeal.

Regardless of the vagaries of its mandate, the special review panel delivered findings based on forty-four public meetings conducted during the summer, along with 650 direct presentations and 35,259 responses to an associated online questionnaire.[3] It framed its findings in the form of questions, and exhorted the federal government to consider those questions before accepting the NEB recommendation. The two most important: "Can construction of a new Trans Mountain Pipeline be reconciled with Canada's climate change commitments?" and "How might Cabinet square approval of the Trans Mountain Pipeline with its commitment to reconciliation with First Nations and to the UNDRIP [UN Declaration on the Rights of Indigenous Peoples] principles of 'free, prior, and informed consent'?" The first was entirely legitimate, a call for a genuine rationalization of national climate policy to Canada's growing its hydrocarbon production sector, although the panel offered no substantive guidance on how to do that. In respect of the second question, the panel conceded that the various First Nations proximate to the pipeline had differing positions on the project, some supportive, some opposed. The panel reaffirmed that public reactions in Alberta and the B.C. interior were starkly different from those closer to Burnaby. An affirmation of the obvious, to be sure.

Whatever utility the Trudeau government expected from this panel was difficult to discern. On its face, the report provided enough questions to allow the government to reconsider the NEB's recommendation, but it did not cite specific technical deficiencies in the NEB process, nor did it address Environment Canada's climate impact assessment.

Regardless, within a few days of its release in early November Trudeau provided the final substantive preliminary to a decision on TMX. He announced a $1.5 billion ocean-protection plan for responses to tanker and fuel spills in the Pacific, Atlantic, and Arctic Oceans. Improved spill response was of course one of B.C. premier Clark's five conditions for any oil sands pipeline project terminating on the B.C. coast, and she responded that she was now satisfied with the plan.

On November 29 the Trudeau government formally approved TMX. Alberta's quid pro quo was finally delivered. Notley kept up her end of the bargain: she voiced no critique of the loss of Northern Gateway, was all in on the Pan-Canadian Framework, and would implement coal shutdown in Alberta. Now Trudeau had seemingly kept up his end of the bargain as well.

A few weeks after Trudeau's approval, Kinder Morgan tied up a last loose end, namely providing Clark with enough additional financial compensation for her B.C. government to accept the project. Once the project was in operation, the province would receive as much as $1 billion over the following two decades. It would receive yearly payments of at least $25 million and, depending on volumes, up to $50 million. That payment would be derived from a surcharge applied to shippers. "The project has met the five conditions," Clark proclaimed. The B.C. NDP condemned the approval and Clark's acquiescence, notwithstanding that the federal government would provide the province with significant additional financial compensation and spending on spill response.

NDP leader John Horgan vowed, if elected, to stop the project, even though this same position had contributed to his party's 2013 election defeat by Clark's Liberals. In the months leading up to the May 2017 B.C. election, TMX continued work to satisfy the NEB conditions, add further Indigenous support via consensual benefit agreements, and progress final internal approvals for the project. That process culminated on May 25, 2017, when Kinder Morgan announced that it had secured sufficient financing to commence construction. That financing would involve spinning off its Canadian subsidiary, Kinder Morgan Canada Limited, and the issue of 102.9 million shares at $17 a share, for total gross proceeds of $1.75 billion. Kinder Morgan would retain a 70 percent ownership in its Canadian subsidiary.

In the May 2017 provincial election, the B.C. Liberal Party won the largest number of seats of any party, but the NDP only won two fewer seats, with a total of forty-one. The Green Party won three. On May 29 the NDP and Green Party entered into an agreement that toppled the Clark Liberals. Whatever pragmatic attributes Horgan may have had, those were quashed by the terms of his commitment to Green Party leader Andrew Weaver to "immediately employ every tool available" to stop TMX. Implacable opposition would typify the provincial government's approach to the project. Within weeks, the B.C. government sought status in the litigation launched by First Nations and municipalities to stop the project.[4] As legal adviser to these obstructionist initiatives, Horgan engaged Thomas Berger, the eighty-four-year-old former B.C. Supreme Court justice and long-time NDP politician most famous for his 1975 report on pipeline development in the Mackenzie Valley — a report that set back any development for generations. The move may have been mostly symbolic, but it clearly resonated with Horgan's political base.

For much of the next nine months, into the spring of 2018, the TMX project team tried to advance construction, particularly around the Burnaby terminal, doing additional survey work, ground sampling, and other types of route preparation. The City of Burnaby made this as difficult as possible by slow-walking what would have been, in the normal course of events, a routine issuance of various municipal permits for access. The Horgan government professed that it would not artificially delay permits for TMX, despite the premier's vow to use every available tool to stop the project, but in late October of 2017 Burnaby's obstruction, aided by Horgan's acquiescence, compelled Kinder Morgan to disclose publicly that the coastal city of Burnaby had not provided the required permits, and that the company would appeal to the NEB for alternative permissions.

This action was necessary, Kinder Morgan held, to preserve the project's in-service date of late 2019. According to Canadian constitutional law, in the event of an operational conflict between federal approval and a provincial law or municipal bylaw, the federal approval prevails. But the question remained: How much further delay must infrastructure endure before the NEB developed a process to provide permission in lieu of municipal and provincial authorities? In early December 2017 the NEB allowed TMX to bypass municipal and provincial authorities in respect of some permits, and on January 18 it launched a generic process to resolve permissions issues between Kinder Morgan Canada and provincial and municipal authorities, demonstrating that the regulator and courts were willing to sustain the federal approval. How efficient these workaround processes would prove, at least in the context of the existing project timeline, remained an open question.

On January 30, 2018, British Columbia announced its intention to pursue a "second phase" of environmental regulations, to be promulgated as early as 2019. This second phase would concern itself with pipeline safety and spill response, as well as restrictions on transporting diluted bitumen through British Columbia. Furthermore, the province intended to submit a reference question to the courts regarding its authority to enact additional legislation regulating potential environmental impacts of diluted bitumen and other heavy oils. In other words, if it succeeded, British Columbia would force a new, redundant, multiyear environmental review process on TMX, throwing in doubt the paramountcy of federal jurisdiction. Whatever the outcome of this effort, the Horgan government had already created a new legal risk for the project.

Over the first quarter of 2018, TMX obtained from the federal courts injunctive relief from various protestors assaulting their Burnaby terminal. Despite that, some protests persisted, culminating in hundreds of arrests, including the arrests of prominent leftist politicians such as Elizabeth May, the leader of the federal Green Party, and Stewart Kennedy, a Burnaby-area NDP MP. Trudeau had publicly demonstrated his own commitment to the project in February, when he confronted hecklers at the famous town hall meeting in Nanaimo, enduring the indignities as part of his implicit deal with Alberta and asserting his conviction that TMX was in the Canadian national interest, compatible with the country's carbon goals. Less encouragingly, the federal government did not publicly denounce Horgan's obstructionist tactics. The Trudeau government's ambiguous signals had already been demonstrated by Energy Minster Jim Carr in December 2017, when he contended that he would use whatever means necessary to prevent obstruction of TMX and then promptly walked back that position by acknowledging Canadians' right to assemble and protest. He provided no guidance, however, on the line between lawful protest and outright illegal obstruction. The leadership of Kinder Morgan certainly took that into account.

By the end of March 2018 TMX had obtained approvals from NEB, sustained by the federal courts and by prominent municipal authorities, however ponderously. Kinder Morgan had spent close to a $1 billion; still, the highest ranks of the Kinder Morgan organization wondered if persisting with the project still made economic sense. The Horgan government seemed likely to launch additional jurisdictional challenges, and to join Burnaby in other obstructionist tactics. Legal claims were, meanwhile, still working through the Federal Court of Appeal process. The business case for the project was still robust, based on continuing shipper commitment and the decreasing received value by Alberta producers for Canadian diluted bitumen as a result of the lack of sufficient additional pipeline capacity. But if the project could not actually be built, the business case meant nothing.

The Federal Court of Appeal dismissed British Columbia's appeal to stop the NEB from supplying permits in lieu of municipal ones, and the City of Burnaby immediately challenged that decision, taking it to the Supreme Court of Canada. Notably, as of the end of March 2018 Kinder Morgan had never yet lost in the Canadian courts, and the TMX approval remained credible, backed so far by federal institutions.

Nevertheless, on March 6, 2018, representatives of Kinder Morgan met with Minister Carr and his chief of staff, Zoë Caron, in Houston, Texas, where they laid out new demands for the Canadian government to meet. According to a preliminary proxy statement for shareholders, for Kinder Morgan to proceed with TMX, the Trudeau government would have to provide

1. clarity and certainty on the paramountcy of federal approvals, including legislation that would provide a "once and for all" approval of the federally approved undertakings, rendering British Columbia's initiatives to stop the project ineffective; and
2. a financial backstop arrangement that would keep Shareholders whole in the event of a stoppage or suspension of the [Trans Mountain expansion project].

Through the remainder of March, Kinder Morgan's negotiations with the government continued, including with officials from the Department of Finance and the Prime Minister's Office. As additional consideration, if the federal government acceded to Kinder Morgan's demands, Kinder offered it the option to purchase a 5 percent ownership interest if the project were placed into service. Not surprisingly, federal officials responded to Kinder Morgan's aggressive demand by attempting to limit the conditions upon which such a backstop could be invoked. The dynamic had Kinder Morgan testing the Trudeau government's commitment to the project. No doubt Kinder Morgan stressed that the Horgan government's implacable opposition posed an untenable risk it was not prepared to accept, even though the election of such a government had always been possible. To increase pressure on the Trudeau government, Kinder Morgan announced publicly on April 8 that it would suspend all non-essential spending on TMX, and that, under current circumstances, including the Government of British Columbia's continued opposition, it would not commit additional shareholder resources to the project. Kinder Morgan set a May 31 deadline for the federal government to work out an acceptable agreement to salvage the project. Otherwise, Kinder Morgan would terminate.

The Trudeau government's immediate reaction was to admonish the Horgan government for having brought on this crisis. Energy Minister Carr stated: "The government of Canada calls on Premier Horgan and the B.C. government to end all threats of delay to the Trans Mountain expansion. His government's actions stand to harm the entire Canadian economy."

Predictably, Horgan was both defensive and defiant: "I want to say to all Canadians that I profoundly believe in the rights of British Columbians to stand up and make sure that we're doing everything we can to protect the interests of our province." He denied that his government had harassed the project unreasonably.

Notley mused about the possibility of Alberta taking an equity position in the project to help salvage it.

With further negotiations about to unfold, Trudeau, Horgan, and Notley met on a Sunday morning, April 15. The net result was no accommodation from Horgan, but an unequivocal declaration by Trudeau that

Prime Minister Justin Trudeau, Alberta premier Rachel Notley, and B.C. premier John Horgan meet to discuss the possibility of salvaging TMX, April 2018.

the pipeline would be built. "The environment and the economy must go together," he declared. Trudeau and Notley were committed to finding some financial accommodation with Kinder Morgan. Neither suggested any retribution against the Horgan government.

Kinder Morgan soon moved to compel the federal government to buy the project outright. The company was no longer interested in any backstop indemnity structure. Federal government negotiators continued holding to the position that the two sides should aim for a mutually acceptable backstop agreement that implicitly conceded the level of risk that had evolved was untenable for Kinder Morgan to accept, and at least justified some level of federal financial indemnity. The indemnity offer was reasonable, from the government's perspective, if it believed the risks Kinder Morgan found untenable would not ultimately come to pass, and that the Canadian judicial system would uphold both federal paramountcy and the existing federal approval. Moreover, the Trudeau government was fully prepared to deal efficiently with any future obstructions, whether in the form of civil disobedience or legal action.

Finance Minister Bill Morneau and Natural Resources Minister Jim Carr explain the federal government's decision to purchase TMX.

By early May, Finance Minister Bill Morneau was directly involved in the negotiations. He continued to offer Kinder Morgan a limited indemnity.[5] If Kinder Morgan abandoned the project for certain specified reasons or could not complete the project by a certain date, the indemnity provided by the federal government would also cover certain costs spent up to that point. Morneau put in play the prospect of offering the TMX project, including the federal indemnity, to third parties. Much to the disappointment of the Trudeau government, however, no plausible third-party entity such as TransCanada or Enbridge came forward to acquire the project.

Within a week Kinder Morgan outright rejected any indemnity-based accommodation. The only acceptable option for Kinder Morgan was for the federal government to purchase both TMX and the original Trans Mountain pipeline — otherwise Kinder Morgan would terminate the project. Kinder Morgan was playing hardball. On May 22 the Trudeau government conceded that the parties could not negotiate an indemnity arrangement. It would follow the only path left to sustain the project. The Trudeau government was not prepared to call Rich Kinder's bluff; it was not prepared to lose TMX. Morneau could only pursue the best price possible.

Over the next forty-eight hours, Morneau and Kinder Morgan came to an agreed purchase price of $4.5 billion. However, Kinder Morgan would pay $325 million of capital gains taxes upon closing, effectively reducing the net price to $4.175 billion. This was a substantial premium beyond the value of the existing Trans Mountain system and the assets represented by the $1 billion already spent on TMX: a premium on the order of $1 to 1.5 billion. The premium would be recoverable only if the project proceeded and expanded, in terms of both its capacity and its tariff structure.

By the end of May 2018, Trudeau had unarguably fulfilled his part of the quid pro quo he had negotiated with Notley. He had intervened to the extent of $4.5 billion — an intervention no one had foreseen even a few months earlier. No doubt Cabinet struggled to accept the purchase; accepting market access for Canadian diluted bitumen through a regulatory approval was one thing, but expending $4.5 billion was quite another. Furthermore, the decision would only further strain voter faith in the government's commitment to national climate targets.

Not surprisingly, Morneau took the lead in justifying the transaction, calling it "of vital interest to Canada and Canadians." He stated, "Our government's position is clear: It must be built and it will be built." Notley demonstrated palpable relief, akin to a survivor of a near-death experience. The only remaining pipeline within Canadian jurisdiction had been salvaged. Her political collaboration with Trudeau still held.

The transaction would close in late August, and with it a transition of TMX executives and staff from Kinder Morgan to some still-to-be-defined legal entity owned by the federal government. For the ENGO world and the B.C. government, a change of ownership changed nothing; they remained implacably opposed to the project. Canadian public opinion was relatively evenly split on the TMX purchase, while a majority supported the concept of providing market access. From a purely political perspective, the Liberal Party saw little, if any, erosion of its national support. Morneau had done as well as anyone could have, given the situation. The government had lost leverage with Kinder Morgan when it lost Energy East and rejected Northern Gateway, and it was not prepared to rely solely on a revived KXL and Enbridge Line 3. The last Canadian-controlled market access option had to remain in play, even to the incredible extremity of nationalizing a project that should have been realized, given its economics, conventional technology, and manageable spill risk, by the private sector.[6]

In the summer of 2018, Notley made a show of her optimism by posing for photographs with federal energy minister Amarjeet Sohi and TMX chief executive Ian Anderson, putting shovels into the ground west of Edmonton to commence construction. TMX, the images implied, was inevitable. But on August 30, just after 8:30 Mountain Standard Time, the unthinkable happened. The day before the Trudeau government would send $4.5 billion to Kinder Morgan to close the acquisition, the Federal Court of Appeal intervened, and shocked both the Trudeau and Notley governments to the core.

Tsleil-Waututh Nation v. Canada (Attorney General) was the product of consolidated action by various First Nations, municipalities, and ENGOs, and it represented the final major legal challenge to the project's approval. Few expected it to prevail. But on August 30, 2018, the Federal Court of Appeal nullified the approval of TMX on two grounds. First, it ruled that the NEB's scoping decision to exclude the increased marine traffic needed to be addressed. Second, it ruled that the federal government had not adequately discharged its duty to consult and accommodate affected Indigenous Peoples over the period following the NEB's recommendation for government approval. The project was immediately suspended until these deficiencies were remedied.

The court did dismiss the vast majority of the claims against the NEB. These included allegations that the hearings were procedurally unfair because the intervenors had inadequate opportunity to cross-examine Kinder Morgan, and that the NEB had failed to consider alternatives to the Westridge Marine Terminal. But in the words of Mercutio in Shakespeare's *Romeo and Juliet*: "'Tis enough."

A huge setback to TMX. This project, which the Trudeau government had identified as in the public interest, this cornerstone of balance between energy and climate policy, was potentially undone.

● ● ● ● ●

With its first cited deficiency — failure to include impacts of increased tanker traffic resulting from the pipeline expansion in the scope of its environmental assessment — the Federal Court of Appeal revisited a fundamental scoping decision made almost five years earlier. The NEB's view was that marine impacts fell outside its jurisdiction and would be assessed and mitigated by the Department of Transport. By the NEB's logic, it could not impose conditions on marine traffic without jurisdiction over marine shipping, so though it accepted and considered evidence on marine impacts, it left the mitigation to departments with that jurisdiction. But the court held that the NEB failed to provide a reasonable basis for excluding marine traffic from the scope of review, and it now required the NEB to complete the assessment and to determine appropriate conditions to mitigate impacts. The court also observed that by failing to scope in marine effects, the NEB allowed the federal government potentially to avoid direct accountability for dealing with potential adverse impacts, particularly the impact on orcas in Burrard Inlet.

The second deficiency related to consultations carried out by the federal government during the six months after the NEB had issued its recommendation for approval and before Trudeau's final decision to accept that recommendation, on November 29, 2016. This was essentially a repeat of the judgment rendered against Northern Gateway back in May 2016. The Federal Court of Appeal condemned the Trudeau government for having its officials merely listen passively to the concerns of Indigenous groups and document those concerns for later consideration. The court expected, instead, a negotiation that addressed concerns and led to consensual accommodation, and to that end, it cited evolving Supreme Court of Canada and Federal Court of Appeal precedent on expected standards of consultation.

The court professed that its decision did not provide a de facto Indigenous veto. Rather: "What is required is a process of balancing interests — a process of give and take. Nor does consultation equate to a duty to agree; rather, what is required is a commitment to a meaningful process of consultation."

Rachel Notley responds with anger and frustration in her speech following the Federal Court of Appeal's decision to suspend approval of the TMX project.

This decision emphasized a new standard on the federal government "to grapple." What did that mean? The wording was far too ambiguous to translate into practical guidance on the nature of adequate accommodation or consultation, or on the authority of the federal government to make a final decision. Moreover, the decision showed no recognition of the broader public interest in terms of lost value from the project, future impact on investment in Canada, or fairness to proponents.

TMX was immediately suspended. The federal government, now both the project proponent and the party with the duty to consult, would have to try to rectify these deficiencies before the approval could be restored, although there was no guarantee that such attempted rectification would ultimately pass muster with the Federal Court of Appeal, or with the Supreme Court, for that matter. Nevertheless, the following day, the Canadian government followed through on the acquisition from Kinder Morgan, with a payment of $4.5 billion.

For Notley, Alberta, and the oil sands industry, the decision was devastating. Notley's public remarks a few hours after the decision reflected the overwhelming attitude of dismay and anger: "Albertans are angry. I am angry.... Alberta has done everything right and we have been let down.... It is a crisis." She did not provide any specific critique of the decision in legal terms. Instead, she indicated that Alberta would pull out of the Pan-Canadian Framework climate change plan, although that would not impact the existing provincial carbon tax. In essence, future carbon-price increases laid out in the federal climate plan were off the table for Alberta until market access was rectified. This anguished response simply demonstrated the obvious, that Alberta was in the hands of the Trudeau government, and could only wait and see how it would respond to the Federal Court of Appeal decision. Notley was justifiably forlorn.

So, what were the Trudeau government's plausible responses? First, it could appeal the decision to the Supreme Court of Canada, a process that would take a year to run its course, with no certainty of success. Second, it could comply with the Federal Court of Appeal and remedy the deficiencies, despite the time required, and then potentially face litigation again. This process would likely cause as much delay as the appeal route.

The third option was a legislative response. The Trudeau government could simply reissue TMX's approval with new conditions to deal with marine impacts, specifically the orcas in Burrard Inlet, and with additional accommodations to address, perhaps only in part, the concerns raised by Indigenous groups in the 2016 consultation. Construction could recommence relatively quickly, although the project would still be vulnerable to legal challenges to the Supreme Court. This approach would have worked around, or served as a compromise for, further consultation exercises with specific First Nations as set out in the Federal Court of Appeal judgment of August 31. But this legislation could have imposed new conditions on the project that would assuage, at least in part, some of the outstanding grievances cited by the court. Only this third option could avoid protracted delay, despite its vulnerability to future litigation and near-term attempts at injunctive relief by opponents of the project.

Over the next month, the Trudeau government deliberated. Not surprisingly, it opted to pursue the remedy option. Specifically, on September 20, 2018, the Government of Canada directed the NEB to complete a reconsideration of the marine issues cited in its August 31 decision, and to report back no later than February 22, 2019. A few weeks later it announced: "The Government will not appeal the FCA decision." Consultations with First Nations resumed, and Trudeau appointed former Supreme Court of Canada justice the Honourable Frank Iacobucci as a federal representative to oversee the consultation process and help it comply with the appeal court's decision. But the government provided no guidance, publicly, on how long this consultation process could run. Persevering with remedying the Federal Court of Appeal decision was the only solace for Alberta, and brought no guarantee that the province's demand for market access would ever be satisfied with a pipeline entirely within Canadian jurisdiction.

Sadly, TMX went into hiatus, likely to extend into midyear 2019. The last all-Canadian large-scale pipeline option had been set back by judicial review, with no apparent regard for the broader public interest. Even with the Trudeau government's 2016 approval and $4.5 billion of taxpayer money to preserve it, TMX could not get to construction by the end of 2018. Amazingly, this government that had made reconciliation with First Nations a defining initiative had been unable to follow the 2016 dictate of the Federal Court of Appeal on the Northern Gateway project on what constituted adequate consultation — a sad irony.

CHAPTER 6

Late 2018: Blows on a Bruise

TMX, THE LAST CANADIAN-CONTROLLED market access option, drifted into an indeterminate remedy process as 2018 closed out. The Notley government rationalized that other pipeline options still validated their future budget assumptions around increased oil sands production and resulting cash flows, but those options had been whittled down to the Enbridge Line 3 expansion, which offered no more than 300,000 barrels per day, and KXL, the material option, with its capacity of over 800,000 barrels per day. Line 3 had achieved its final regulatory requirement, approval from Minnesota's Public Utilities Commission, in June 2018; however, a month later, various First Nations bands and environmental groups filed three separate lawsuits against the Public Utilities Commission, asking the Minnesota Court of Appeals to overturn the commission's May 2018 decision that found Line 3's environmental impact statement "adequate." These lawsuits were largely ignored in conversations about Line 3 within Canada, but still constitute continuing risk to whether the line will begin operations by the end of 2019.

Meanwhile, on November 8, 2018, just as TransCanada was poised to ramp up pre-construction activities for KXL in Montana, a federal court judge in that state issued a ruling that nullified Trump's permit for KXL to cross the U.S.-Canada border. The lawsuit had been filed in

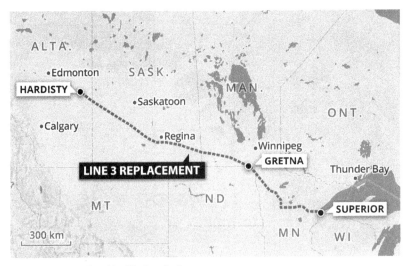

Source: Mapbox, OpenStreetMap; The Canadian Press
Line 3 Route

March 2017 by the Northern Plains Resource Council, Bold Alliance, the Center for Biological Diversity, Friends of the Earth, the Natural Resources Defense Council, and the Sierra Club. It challenged the Trump administration, the U.S. Department of State, and various government agencies, alleging that the pipeline's environmental review, which relied on an environmental impact statement from January 2014, was inadequate and outdated, and failed to consider key information on the project's impacts. U.S. District Court Judge Brian Morris ordered the federal government to conduct a more thorough environmental analysis, opining that the administration had failed to present a "reasoned explanation" for the move and "simply discarded" the effect the project would have on climate change. The ruling blocked construction until such time as these deficiencies were remedied.

"It was a political decision made by a judge," was Trump's reaction. "I think it's a disgrace." This same judge, an Obama appointee, had already forced TransCanada to carry out more environmental assessment of the reroute through Nebraska, as specified by that state's Public Utilities Commission. TransCanada had completed a 338-page report dealing with that demand.

Three options remained for TransCanada and the Trump administration: appeal, comply with the ruling, or find some executive-order workaround to the ruling. The appeal option would be problematic given the leftist political orientation of the San Francisco–based Ninth Circuit Court of Appeals, and due to the time required for further appeal to the United States Supreme Court. Still, the ruling's contention that the "department … simply discarded prior factual findings related to climate change to support its course reversal" was curious given that the Department of State's 2014 Final Environmental Impact Statement for KXL had found the project's reasonably attributable incremental emissions "immaterial."[1] How long would a supplemental assessment take to complete? And would a new Department of State permit based on such a supplemental assessment still be litigated by the project's implacable opponents? Furthermore, there was the question of whether the project could be completed within Donald Trump's first term as president. If the project was not completed until 2021, it could be vulnerable to a certainly more hostile Democratic administration. By year's end, TransCanada was still assessing its options, but continued to assert its commitment to the project. The Notley and Trudeau governments expressed disappointment but continued to show deference to the U.S. process.

Within days of the ruling, Cenovus, one of Canada's largest oil sands producers, called publicly for the Alberta government to impose crude oil production cuts in order to improve overall revenues to Alberta oil sands producers.[2] Throughout 2018 total crude oil production within Alberta continued to grow, increasing the imbalance between production volumes and available pipeline capacity, which forced producers to accept additional discounts in price for their crude, as downstream refineries ruthlessly exploited that imbalance. By November 15, 2018, West Texas Intermediate — the key North American benchmark for oil prices — rose to about US$56.80 for December delivery. Canada's heavy-oil benchmark, in contrast, continued its recent slide and hit a record low that week, trading at US$13.46 a barrel.[3] Constraining aggregate production by collectivizing Alberta crude production would create more bargaining leverage with refining interests.

Of course, a few Alberta crude producers owned crude oil refineries accessible to Alberta supply, and they captured very significant margin improvement. They would not likely endorse such a concept. Obviously, the plan would require allocating production allowances to specific Alberta producers, a process that would be contentious and could take a long time to implement. The Province of Alberta is a major crude oil producer via its royalty share, and had the greatest interest in increasing aggregate revenues by whatever mechanism possible in the short run — admittedly, a long "short run" that could extend into 2021. That it would even consider implementing production cuts showed just how desperate the situation had become; the aggregate value loss, it contended, was on the order of $50 million to $60 million per day.[4]

Different commentators and analysts would estimate the economic impact somewhat differently, depending on specific assumptions about the duration and quantity of the discount. But if the level of the discount endured in November 2018 persisted over twelve months, Canadian interests, including producers and the Alberta and Canadian treasuries, stood to lose cash flow approaching $15 billion a year. For context, Alberta's operating deficit that year was on the order of $8 billion, and the projected federal deficit was $18 billion. Canada would inevitably lose future investment in future production as well, if all market access options were closed off.

As Alberta and Canada saw the real consequences of market access frustration in the form of these price discounts, just as predictably the ENGO community took a victory lap. CorpEthics, a strategic adviser to environmental campaigns and strategic partner with the Sierra Club, Natural Resources Defense Council, and 350.org, issued a representative statement: "From the very beginning, the campaign strategy was to land-lock the tar sands so their crude could not reach the international market where it could fetch a high price per barrel. This meant national and grassroots organizing to block all proposed pipelines. This strategy is successful to this day."[5]

That summation overreached a little, but at the end of 2018 all of the past decade's pipeline projects to market access had been terminated or caught up in indeterminate legal and political approval processes. At year end, the Trudeau government offered sympathy for Alberta, but nothing else. It persisted with C-69, continued its consultations on TMX, and remained committed to implausible emissions reduction targets.

On December 3, Notley announced an 8.7 percent production cut, roughly 350,000 barrels per day, to be implemented on January 1, 2019. It would remain in place at that level at least until existing surplus inventories were processed, which was projected to occur by the spring of 2019. The production cuts would gradually be reduced over 2019, and Notley intended to eliminate them by the end of that year, coincident with the in-service date of the Enbridge Line 3 expansion. The Alberta government expected margin improvement on the order of $4 per barrel. Notley described the cuts as "difficult but necessary." The Alberta production industry's reaction was predictably divided between those with significant downstream refinery positions and those without. But even those opposed to Notley's intervention acquiesced without any significant public comment. Even Alberta's United Conservative Party official opposition supported the plan in an extraordinary, almost unprecedented, bipartisan demonstration of alignment, given the extremity of the discounts being endured. The Notley government also stated its intention to pursue the purchase of additional rail cars and locomotives to increase transportation capacity by an additional 120,000 barrels per day.

As this unfolded in Alberta, the Trump administration released its mandated national climate assessment late in November. The report confirms that it is extremely likely that human activities, especially emissions of greenhouse gases, are the dominant cause of the observed warming since the mid-twentieth century. For the warming over the last century, the assessment concludes, the observational evidence supports no convincing alternative explanation.

The document also contends that without more significant mitigation efforts, there will be substantial damages to the U.S. economy, human health, and the environment. Under scenarios with high emissions and limited or no adaptation, annual losses in some sectors are estimated to grow to hundreds of billions of dollars by the end of the century.[6]

Thirteen federal agencies authored the report, with the National Oceanic and Atmospheric Administration serving as its lead coordinator. It contains no specific policy recommendation.

At roughly the same time, the UN released its Emissions Gap Report, reaffirming that existing commitments from the Paris Climate Accord are not consistent with containing the temperature increase at 1.5 degrees Celsius: "If NDC [nationally determined contributions for reductions in greenhouse gas emissions] ambitions are not increased before 2030, exceeding the 1.5°C goal can no longer be avoided ... in fact, global CO_2 emissions increased in 2017 after three years of stagnation.... Global greenhouse gas emissions show no signs of peaking."[7]

As the delegates convened at a UN climate meeting in Katowice, Poland, in early December, riots broke out in France in response to the Macron government's imposition of higher fuel taxes to discourage fossil-fuel use. Protests appropriated by various extremists of both the left and the right morphed into violent confrontations and significant property damage over three weekends, primarily in Paris. On December 4, President Macron capitulated and suspended the planned fuel tax hike, promising a three-month national debate on how to fight climate change without hurting French pocketbooks. All this proved yet again how difficult it is for political leaders to impose real, direct costs to deal with the risk of climate change, especially if the regressive impacts of a de facto carbon tax are not in some fashion mitigated.

The prime minister and provincial premiers convened in Montreal just as the world showed Canada, yet again, how difficult it would be to impose stringent climate mitigation policy on current electorates, notwithstanding the UN process's continued insistence on containing world temperature increase within 1.5 to 2.0 degrees Celsius. The federal government resisted devoting the entire day-and-a-half meeting solely to pipelines and carbon policy, despite the urgency of the situation in Alberta, and despite resistance to the federal carbon pricing standard from Saskatchewan, Ontario, Manitoba, and New Brunswick. The provinces aired their grievances but effected no change in existing federal policy.

This was hardly surprising, given that just a week earlier Trudeau had held a public meeting in Calgary, immediately following his government's

Justin Trudeau speaks at a meeting of the Calgary Chamber of Commerce, November 2018.

fiscal update, and announced empathy but no federal action to either deal with the discount issue or accelerate the process on restoring TMX to construction. Instead, he offered condescending truisms: "You think there's a super-simple easy answer and there's not." He continued: "There's a multifaceted complex issue and as much as there is a tendency out there in the world to give really simple answers to really complex questions, unfortunately the world doesn't work like that. We need to make sure that we're moving forward in the right way and that is where actually listening to the experts is sort of the best way to make policy."

Even more insulting to Albertans, Quebec premier François Legault commented, in response to the possibility of reviving the Energy East project, that he saw no "social acceptability" for moving Alberta's "dirty oil" through Quebec. Legault did not elaborate on what defined "dirty oil" or "social acceptability." Of course, he did not acknowledge the reality that the Energy East project fell under federal jurisdiction, over which Quebec presumably held no veto. Nor did he admit that Quebec would receive $1.4 billion more in equalization payments for

2019, while Alberta was still deemed a "have" province, given the mechanics of the equalization process. All of this was beyond insufferable to Alberta — hobbled by the frustration of market access over the past decade, unprecedented price discounts reducing cash flow into the province, unctuous comments from Quebec on "dirty oil," and more process and ambiguity from the Trudeau government.

Amazingly, this insufferable situation was made even worse when Trudeau essentially conceded to Quebec a veto on any revival of Energy East. In an end-of-year interview with CTV, Evan Solomon asked if Trudeau was open to revitalizing an Energy East pipeline, and Trudeau responded: "There is no project on the table. The proponent has walked away."

Solomon persisted: "But if the government came forward to de-risk it as you did with Trans Mountain, maybe you'd get a proponent?"

Trudeau's response: "You can't de-risk in an absence of a project, and there is clarity that under the current approach there is no support for a pipeline through Quebec."

In other words, he chose to ignore the paramountcy of the federal regulatory process and considerations of national benefits, and he did not dispute the contention of "dirty oil." Of course, the Liberal Party depended on seventy-five seats in the Province of Quebec to preserve its majority in the next federal election.

The year closed out with federal Natural Resources Minister Sohi announcing to Albertans that an additional $1.5 billion would be granted to the Export Development Corporation and the Business Development Bank of Canada to provide loans for the oil and gas sector — an underwhelming initiative. Notley appropriately captured the attitude of Albertans: "We didn't ask for the opportunity to go further into debt as a means of addressing this problem."

As for any fundamental change to the process to restore TMX to construction, Sohi had nothing to offer.[8]

Just at the end of 2018 and into early January 2019, resistance to the LNG Canada project and its gas supply pipeline, Coastal Gas Link, came to a head. A group of hereditary chiefs of the Wet'suwet'en Nation had maintained a blockade for over four years at a critical river crossing just east of the coastal mountains, while the project had achieved consensual agreements with the vast majority of Indigenous entities along the pipeline, including the elected leadership of the Wet'suwet'en. TransCanada, owner and operator of Coastal Gas link, achieved a court ruling to have the blockade removed, and that ruling was enforced by the RCMP. Subsequently, the leadership struck an interim agreement with the protesters, who agreed to comply with an interim court injunction that granted workers temporary entry to the area. The group remained, however, "adamantly opposed" to the project. Predictably, coordinated protests ensued in various Canadian locales, with equally predictable media coverage full of affecting visuals and superficial analysis of the legalities in play. Does Canadian law mean anything anymore?

Not surprisingly, Shell executives responsible for LNG Canada ominously intoned that any further delays in the project could erode confidence in the ability of British Columbia and Canada to deliver energy projects. No doubt about that. Trudeau and Horgan, back in October, had participated with beaming smiles at the event marking an affirmative decision to proceed with the project, and they doubtless felt special agony around enforcement, given all of their past rhetoric on reconciliation. Horgan, especially, had adamantly resisted the use of the B.C. coast by oil sands pipelines, and had implicitly aligned with similar Indigenous resistance at the TMX terminal at Burnaby. Now he found himself called upon to salvage LNG in British Columbia by enforcing the rights of the project.

TransCanada persisted with efforts to gain the consent required to access the river-crossing infrastructure. This resembled its efforts of the previous four years in the face of the same kinds of resistance from the same sources, except the entire project now hung in the balance. How was it to deal with an entity adamantly opposed to the project, one that contends it is not subject to Canadian law? Ultimately, Canada has to enforce its collective interests. Would Horgan and Trudeau be up to that?

The year 2018 was, for Alberta, an *annus horribilis*, to be sure.

PART TWO

Solutions

CHAPTER 7

Finding a Way

CANADIAN HYDROCARBON PRODUCTION contributes about 5 percent of the total Canadian GDP,[1] and if we include related industries that form part of its total value chain, that value approaches 10 percent.[2] In export terms, hydrocarbons comprise roughly 20 percent of total Canadian goods exports,[3] a value of almost $100 billion. However one relates to these statistics, the reality is that hydrocarbons are a major component of the Canadian economy, and their contribution would be difficult, if not impossible, to replace in the short and medium term, if ever.

Despite this, some Canadians remain implacably opposed to the exploitation of this resource. That opposition may or may not become politically dominant in Canada, but its existence brings to my mind a question, one that I expect is also on the minds of most intellectually honest Albertans: Does Canada still work for Alberta?

The province's economic interests depend on developing its hydrocarbon resources on reasonable terms, which in turn requires functional federal processes and some level of national political consensus that hydrocarbon production growth will be part of Canada's economic future. As the events laid out in Part One attest, those prerequisites have substantially broken down. Canada's legal, regulatory, and political systems cannot, evidently, sustain the approval of projects validated economically both by long-term contractual commitments of credit-worthy parties and by enduring global demand for the product the projects would have carried. These projects were to utilize conventional technology, traverse manageable geographies, and conform to the construction and operating standards evolved over time by credible regulators. The proponents would provide compensations and accommodations for impacted stakeholders, well within expected standards. In fact, they had achieved alignment with many, though not all, affected First Nations, through specific benefit agreements. Most of these projects had achieved regulatory recommendations for approval and explicit approvals from the democratically elected governments of their day. But over the past ten years, Canada has achieved no additional pipeline capacity for its oil sands production potential.

Even more incredibly, the TMX project, which in effect was one term of the quid pro quo between Notley and Trudeau — credible Alberta carbon policy for at least one major oil sands pipeline — could not evade the indeterminate cycle of supplemental assessment and additional consultation mandated by the Federal Court of Appeal, apparently indifferent to the enormous economic value at stake, and to the overall context of prior regulatory and political sanction, including past consultation and accommodation efforts. After several years of regulatory process and hundreds of millions of dollars spent, approvals proved meaningless, easily undone after the fact by courts motivated by an agenda as much political as legal. The Trudeau government could have been more aggressive, legislating construction to resume even as it worked to comply with the deficiencies cited by the Federal Court of Appeal, but it did not. It clearly knew the stakes but chose not to confront the decision even to the extent of mounting an appeal, let alone resorting to a legislative response. Trudeau's government expressed no outrage or disappointment, but instead tepidly acquiesced, with an open-ended intention to remedy the court's cited flaws, even as Canada's daily losses in cash flow reached historic levels. The court's decision and the Trudeau government's response demonstrated just how dysfunctional Canada has become, especially in terms of Alberta's interests.

Will the current federal remedy process culminate in TMX getting to construction in 2019? Or even 2020? Or will it evolve into an endless "do loop" of litigation and consultation? The Trump administration and the U.S. legal system might yet restore KXL to construction in 2019, and Enbridge Line 3 might also complete its construction. LNG Canada could also move on to construction. If the past ten years provide any indicator, we should be skeptical. These projects could still face further litigation and inadequate responses to obstruction. Make no mistake: this would be a horrific circumstance for Canada, and especially for Alberta.

But, as we move forward, Canada will endure, with or without a growing economic contribution from its hydrocarbon resources. If that contribution is valued and expected to grow, then what must change? It is a simple question with a three-fold answer. First, the approval process requires fundamental change, even in its current form, let alone what will pertain if Bill C-69 is implemented, a bill that serves substantially the forces of obstruction instead of any reasonable provision of efficiency and fairness to proponents. It cannot be ignored that the environmental movement holds a special animus for Alberta's hydrocarbons because of the oil sands' unique attributes on carbon intensity and the scale of its emissions relative to Canada's existing, implausible carbon targets. Secondly, Canada must, therefore, develop credible and proportionate carbon policy, a policy that does not sacrifice the Canadian hydrocarbon production industry. And finally, Canada must confront fundamental questions about how the statutes governing this country work. Who has veto power over projects, and who doesn't? Does Canada still accept the primacy of the national interest for all Canadians, or will we acquiesce in certain entities' de facto veto power?

The following three chapters offer proposals for how to achieve the necessary changes to address each of the three issues I have identified: the approval process, carbon policy, and specific legislative amendments to clarify significant ambiguities related to First Nations consultation and infringement. Of course, my specific focus remains on hydrocarbons, but these points apply to all major economic development, from electric generation and transmission facilities to non-pipeline transportation infrastructure to major industrial facilities. Can this country provide a rational approval process to deal with projects that create genuine economic opportunity, one that induces private capital to invest? Can we accommodate Canadian carbon policy to additional hydrocarbon production growth? Can we find the political will to enforce approvals?

CHAPTER 8

A Rational Approval Process

TRUDEAU'S STATEMENT THAT HIS GOVERNMENT would strive to be "a referee not a cheerleader" reveals distrust of, if not contempt for, the private sector processes that lead proponents to invest billions of dollars in infrastructure, and the credit-worthy parties prepared to commit long-term to pay for access to such infrastructure. Canada's approval process needs to change, but Bill C-69 is not the answer. Canadian industry's resistance to that legislation speaks for itself. Whatever Trudeau's intent with the bill, it was not designed to fairly and efficiently assess whether projects meet the standard of being in the national interest, and, if so, what conditions, as set by competent and non-ideological regulators, need to be met.

A regulatory approval process cannot ignore that projects of scale and national significance akin to those discussed in Part One seek regulatory approval after extensive private sector validation of their fundamental economics and long-term viability. Real economic value hangs in the balance. No private sector entity will risk the hundreds of millions of dollars required to obtain approval unless it believes that the approval process and its subsequent regulatory oversight are predictable, efficient, and reasonably consistent with past regulatory practice. What follows are the basic concepts that Canada must accept if this country is to restore its approval process for major energy infrastructure projects such that private sector capital will risk using it. Three core principles must be respected.

First, Canadian politicians must accept that any approval process is functionally useless if it fails to attract capital. No private sector entity will expend the large amounts necessary to seek approvals for projects on the scale of those discussed in this book — ever again — without fundamental change. The Trudeau government's contention that C-69 will enable "good" projects — as if the Trudeau government knows a priori what constitutes a "good" project — to proceed is ridiculous, rebutted by the implacable opposition from the very entities Canada relies on to take on such projects.

If the approval process poses so much risk that no private interest would use it, the government would better reject certain development outright rather than persist with the charade of an approval process that proves an insuperable barrier to development. But that requires intellectual honesty. All reasonable centrist Canadian politicians should be able to accept that for any approval process to attract capital to take on its risks, the system must be predictable and efficient, culminating in robust, enforced approvals.

It was once the norm in Canada that approvals led to operating infrastructure. This must become the norm again if the country actually wants development, not simply an assessment process as an end in itself. By predictability, I mean that capital needs to know what kind of development Canada embraces and what kind it doesn't, and it needs to understand standards of compliance and risk tolerance before the fact. By efficiency, I mean not only enforced cycle times, but also that Canada must protect its approvals from frustration after the fact beyond any reasonable standard of due process for rights of appeal, such as revisiting fundamental scoping decisions four years after the fact.

Without this basic condition — that the private sector will actually use it — what is the point of any approval process? That is, other than as a poison pill against development? Modern approval processes for major energy infrastructure are fundamentally technocratic. They set reasonable conditions on operations and construction. They are not focus groups or policy discovery exercises. They are certainly not the appropriate medium for resolving policy. No approval process can function reasonably without objective a priori standards for tolerable environmental impact and stakeholder accommodation. Environmental assessment, meanwhile, is not an end in itself; it has purpose only in the context of proposed development. One can only wonder if the Trudeau government understands that basic reality.

The interests of private capital do not, of course, comprise the national interest, but the willingness of private capital to utilize any national approval process with confidence and trust is a necessary condition to capture economic value when it is available for a country to seize. Or, again, what is the point of the process? Those unwilling to accept this basic principle will learn the hard way, when future capital investment simply does not occur. For lost infrastructure investment, some will continue to blame other factors, from commodity prices to competing alternatives, to invocations of fundamental energy transition. While these are potentially valid and relevant future considerations, they do not obviate the validity of the fundamental principle I have set out here. An approval process that does not work for capital does not work.

Second, the government must provide clarity on policy, and this must occur outside the approval process. It is reasonable to expect the government to clarify specific policy issues relevant to major infrastructure development projects, such that the approval process can proceed in the knowledge of what is or is not government policy. In the context of hydrocarbon development, the federal government's position must not remain ambivalent and ambiguous. Is expanded hydrocarbon production consistent with national climate policy, or is it not? Can Canada tolerate attributable incremental carbon emissions from a specific development project in the context of national emissions reduction ambitions, or can't it? If so, how much more? Every ENGO in North America has insisted that environmental assessments include attributable climate impacts for virtually all hydrocarbon-based energy development, production facilities, and transportation infrastructure; and, more to the point, they insist that we can tolerate no incremental emissions when the whole point of the current UN process is to constrain, if not contract, emissions growth. At least the ENGO expectation is clear. But is that the federal position, too?

In early 2019, in Canada and the United States, there was no explicit prohibition on emissions derived from the production of hydrocarbon emissions, apart from Notley's problematic oil sands emissions cap. C-69 insists on climate assessment as part of its approval process, but with no onus on the government to clarify climate policy to specific development projects. C-69 would turn every approval process into a public debate on the merits for Canada of hydrocarbon production versus emissions reductions, with uncertain prospects of any closure. An approval process is *not* a forum for public policy debate.

Third, any Canadian approval process is constrained by the realities of our evolved law, especially concerning the right to appeal a regulatory decision and concerning what constitutes adequate First Nations consultation and what constitutes justifiable infringement of Aboriginal title or claims to title. But that does not prevent the elected Parliament of Canada from legislating to clarify what those rights represent and what they do not.

With those three core principles as a given, creating a more functional approval process requires first remedying the matters omitted by Bill C-69. Political sanction must come at the beginning of the approval process, not at the end. No longer should proponents be expected to expend hundreds of millions of dollars in an approval process, only to face rejection at the very end of it, often for policy reasons that were evident at the beginning of the process and could have been clarified at the outset. Once this sanction is granted, it cannot be reversed by a subsequent change of government.

The fix is conceptually simple. Any proponent of a major project, but especially those similar to Northern Gateway in terms of scale and interprovincial scope, with significant economic value at stake under federal jurisdiction, should expect clarity from the federal government within twelve months of tabling a preliminary information package on the project's consistency with the national interest. Specifically, the government should provide a definitive response: declare that the project is deemed in the national interest, or simply state that it is not. If it is, the project would still be subject to a second phase of assessment, during which regulators would ultimately establish specific conditions on operations, construction, and stakeholder accommodation. Even with a national interest determination in place, the government could still identify certain environmental or stakeholder impact issues.

The proponent must recognize that the second phase may lead to conditions imposed by the regulator, which may prove problematic. The onus must be on the government of the day, however, not the regulator, to make the determination of national interest. A preliminary information package is not the same as a regulatory filing, but it does contain sufficient description of the project's key elements — technology to be deployed, economic justification, expected mitigable impacts, accommodation principles to third-party stakeholders, consistency with existing federal policy — to inform a national interest determination. It also provides sufficient information to carry out any legally required consultation. Proponents would still face the risk of conditions on operations, construction, and accommodation, but they would not face political risk. The dollars at risk, even within this model, would not be trivial, but would be far fewer than the hundreds of millions that have been lost in recent years.

This fundamental change would have avoided some of the classic dysfunctions of the last ten years. We can imagine an entirely different outcome if the Trudeau government had been bound to respect the Northern Gateway approval and to accept that the national regulatory process had imposed sufficient conditions, consistent with its mandate and with that of the existing environment assessment statutes. Similarly, we can imagine an alternative history to that of the Obama administration's stretching out of KXL's assessment process for almost eight years when rationalizing that an approval lay beyond its political capacity from the outset. Finally, how would a functional regulatory system have dealt with Energy East? The Trudeau government would have been forced to admit as early as possible that it would never impose the project on Quebec without the support of majority public opinion, regardless of how irrational that position might be, and no matter how offensive the notion of national interest subordinated to any province is. Furthermore, if the Trudeau government believed the project to be simply unnecessary, regardless of the private sector's willingness to pay for more market access options, it would have had to make that evident early in the process, not years later. A rational regulatory system would have forced any government to determine whether the project could be rationalized to existing Canadian carbon policy or whether it was prepared to extend an explicit veto to Quebec.

This onus on the federal government to state its position at the beginning of a review process forces policy clarification. Contrast that with the current circumstance under CEAA 2013, and unchanged by Bill C-69, whereby policy clarification comes implicitly embedded, if at all, in the final approval or rejection of a project, after a regulatory recommendation, subsequent to protracted regulatory process. No other change is as important for reinventing the regulatory process so that applicants understand as soon as possible the risk they will undertake with any given application. Even for those who fundamentally oppose development, this construct allows a more transparent and urgent determination of alignment with the public interest, but does not distort the approval process to facilitate procrastination and obstruction.

Some contend that the national interest becomes determinable only at the end of a thorough environmental assessment, but recent experience tells us otherwise. Obama knew he would never approve KXL long before November 2015. He did not clarify his intentions earlier because it was politically expedient not to. For approval processes to stretch out, vulnerable to political rejection inconsistent with the evolving regulatory validation of the project, is simply untenable and unfair. If a project is a non-starter, then the government of the day must clarify that as early as possible. The elephant in the room is obvious. If a federal government wants to reject all hydrocarbon projects on the basis of climate considerations, three or four years of regulatory process will not alter that mindset. If that is not the government's actual position, then it must clarify carbon policy, quantifying allowable incremental attributable emissions. And it must affirm any project's alignment with the national interest as early as possible.

Second, a more functional approval process also requires an onus on the federal government to clarify cumulative-effect issues and to delineate both what it expects of applicants and what applicants can expect from it. Again, the point is to reduce risk for the proponent, making the process as transparent as possible.

A cumulative effect is an impact on the environment caused by the combined results of past, current, and future activities; climate change, then, is the ultimate cumulative effect — atmospheric concentrations of greenhouse gases that accumulate to the point that global temperature changes materially, creating unacceptable impacts. For the major projects discussed in this book, other examples of these effects relate typically to cumulative biodiversity impact, be it on caribou or orcas. But the essential question for an environmental assessment is always the same: For this additional development project, what attributable additional impacts are tolerable?

Think of a linear continuum measuring a cumulative effect, be it species population or pollutant concentration. "As-is" sits at the far left, and at some point to the right we reach the tipping point, beyond which no further additional impact will be tolerated. The proponent is obliged, as it should be, to estimate the additional impact on those measures attributable to the advent of its project. The delta between as-is and the additional impact from the project relative to the tipping point should determine whether the project's additional impact is tolerable. Most importantly, the federal government must define such tipping points, and must do so for known cumulative effects reasonably likely to impact resource development under its jurisdiction for foreseeable major projects, certainly for pipeline and LNG infrastructure. No such onus to provide definitions exists in Bill C-69 or the earlier CEAA 2012. The proponent should not have to do the work of trying to define the tipping point, nor should the environmental assessment process devolve into a discovery process on where that tipping point has been set.

If a project will confront zero tolerance for any additional impact of specific cumulative effect, then the proponent should know that up front. Spill risk, while not always considered a cumulative effect, essentially falls into this category, and can be treated in a conceptually similar manner. The environment assessment asks how much the project's advent would increase attributable risk beyond some limit deemed intolerable, considering existing mitigation and remediation technology.

Proponents should not be expected to estimate impacts that may occur concurrently to their own from other prospective projects, or to forecast other factors that might impact the tipping point. A proponent must estimate its additional impacts and table how its planned mitigations validate that estimate; however, it must not be asked to do so beyond the scope of its own project.

The point is simple. If projects are to face absolute environmental showstoppers, the onus must be on the government to define them before the fact. As an example: if no spill risk is to be countenanced in the Douglas Channel, say so in 2009, before Enbridge applies for Northern Gateway; do not have Enbridge spend hundreds of millions of dollars and achieve at least regulatory sanction with appropriate conditions, only to have that reversed in late 2016 by the political decision of the prime minister. As a final point here, determining a tipping point of environmental impact or an outright showstopper is not solely a scientific enterprise; some level of political judgment will always affect the setting of such limits. Consequently, regulators are not the appropriate entities to make that determination, especially if the limits prove severe enough to negate development entirely for certain geographies. Politicians need to step up and clarify where these limits exist.

As a third condition of a more functional approval process, we need legislative clarity on what constitutes acceptable Indigenous consultation, whether conducted by proponents or by the federal government itself. As well, we need clarity on whether a federal approval, recommended by a national regulator and sanctioned by a democratically elected government, for a major infrastructure project deemed to be in the national interest, is in and of itself adequate justification for infringement of Aboriginal title or even the claim of title. Such an infringement would still require adequate compensation for access, conceptually no different from what applies today to any other Canadian landowner who will not consent to access. Failure to clarify these elements will only haunt any future regulatory process, regardless of how many of the other fundamental reforms are incorporated. There is no escape from the inevitable question: When is an approval ever an approval?

The UN Declaration on the Rights of Indigenous Peoples (UNDRIP) was over twenty-five years in the making. In 2007, 144 states voted in the declaration's favour, and four voted against it — Australia, New Zealand, the United States, and Canada. Canada cited concerns over the stated obligation to obtain "free, prior and informed consent" for any development on ancestral land, and for using resources within an Indigenous population's territory, which could be interpreted as granting veto powers to Indigenous groups. In May 2016, however, the Trudeau government dropped its objector status to the declaration and formally adopted plans to implement it in accordance with the Canadian Constitution. As of 2018 Trudeau had provided no clarity on a plan to do that. Instead, we have seen a succession of rulings by the Supreme Court of Canada and Federal Court of Appeal, trying to rationalize Section 35 of the Canadian Constitution to the approval processes. To date, Canadian courts have tried to define a standard of consultation that ensures, at least in terms of process, good faith negotiations for accommodations by proponents and the federal government with affected First Nations. Of course, this has led to two cases of apparent approvals undone or severely impacted by subsequent judicial rulings, Northern Gateway and TMX.

UNDRIP represents a massive uncertainty for Canadian resource and related infrastructure development. For the present, the federal government has not moved to implement UNDRIP legislatively. Of course it hasn't. How can it ever reconcile "free, prior and informed consent" with "no veto"? As for consultation itself, recent rulings demand much more than the word "consult" seems to imply. The courts expect, instead, proponents and governments to negotiate with Indigenous groups, and to find mutually agreeable terms of accommodation. The courts do not delineate, however, how long such negotiations must continue, even if both parties act in good faith.

Again, consider a spectrum. This one represents two negotiating parties, one of which proposes a course of action that has an impact on the other. A "consultation" clearly involves more than the acting party's informing or providing notice to the affected party. Consultation implies that the proponent seeks out and internalizes the affected party's concerns. Canadian courts, at least in their rulings concerning consultation with Indigenous groups, now expect the acting party not only to explore those matters, but to attempt to find mutually agreeable accommodation of concerns. If mutual agreement is not possible, then the next step depends on who holds what rights vis-à-vis the other. In a negotiation between proponents and an affected stakeholder that is not an Indigenous group, when mutual agreement proves impossible, the regulatory body dictates the outcome, imposing or not imposing project changes on the proponent. If the issue amounts to value provided for access, a special adjudication tribunal sometimes makes the decision. But the matter is resolved financially, in the context of a project that has been approved to proceed. If Indigenous groups do not hold a veto, then presumably the process should not work any differently. If they do hold a veto, then their consent is required. But would such a veto apply in circumstances where outstanding land claims remain unresolved, or to circumstances with treaties in place, or both?

If Indigenous groups hold no veto power, then any consultation, even in the form dictated by recent rulings, must at some point end. If the consultation fails to lead constructively toward some mutually acceptable agreement, when does the federal government have the right to say no? Canada's federal governments have not attempted to legislate objective standards to reduce these ambiguities. Recently, we have seen court rulings second-guess the federal government and proponents' attempts to accommodate First Nations, questioning whether they listened enough and sought solutions constructively. This cannot persist. The federal government must act to reduce this risk in the interests of all Canadians, even if its actions will subsequently be tested in Canadian courts.

The fourth condition for a more functional process is to constrain which matters opponents may refer to judicial review after the government has granted an approval. Legislative action and executive action, including that of regulatory tribunals, require checks and balances, and the judicial review of those deliberations is unnecessary. Historically, courts overturned the deliberations of regulatory tribunals only in the case of egregious fundamental process errors. Until recently, the NEB's history was a long list of decisions mainly sustained over time without reversal. But in August 2018 the Federal Court of Appeal decision intervened in the NEB process decision on TMX, in respect of scoping. Almost five years after the fact, the court nullified the approval and suspended the project. That scoping decision revisited how the national regulator had chosen to deal with TMX's marine impacts, and how it delegated to other federal departments and agencies specific jurisdiction on marine operations in Burrard Inlet. Scoping should be challenged only within a specific time limit, not years after the fact. Moreover, if courts can second-guess scope, where does it end? What if the Federal Court of Appeal decided that the marine impacts extended beyond Burrard Inlet, to the North Pacific Ocean, or that climate effects must be included after all? Again, we require a legislative response to contain such untimely revisiting of fundamental regulatory process decisions.

To move from errors of omission to those of commission, what must the federal government do, at a minimum, to make C-69 tolerable, if that bill must persist into the future? First, consider the climate test. For the last decade, the North American environmental movement has relentlessly demanded that governments impose climate considerations as part of the environmental assessment for any major hydrocarbon infrastructure approval. Centre-left administrations have accommodated that demand. Most notably, the Obama administration imposed such considerations on KXL, which led to the project's first supplemental assessment and the first delay. A second notable example of this pattern is the Trudeau government's acquiescence to the second NEB panel in respect of the Energy East proceeding, allowing it to impose climate considerations long after the original filings — considerations at odds with prior understandings between the federal government, the NEB, and the proponent on scope.

Think of the scene in *Casablanca* when a corrupt police chief, closing the café owned by Humphrey Bogart's character, Rick, under orders from the Gestapo major, declares his shock at finding gambling going on. Just as he says this, an employee steps up and hands the police chief a handful of cash. "Here's your winnings, sir," the employee says — and the chief accepts the money with a thank-you. The same hypocrisy, faux indignation, and self-righteousness abound in government positions on energy projects. Infrastructure that enables additional hydrocarbon production within Canada will increase emissions in absolute terms. Some of those emissions may even prove incremental on a global basis. This is about as revelatory as gambling at Rick's Café.

The government can stipulate at the outset of the approval process that any additional production of oil sands will create incremental emissions within Canada. Canadian oil sands production has higher carbon intensity — emissions per unit of output — than conventional crude oil production, but not substantively more than other heavy oil production alternatives globally. But how many incremental emissions can be attributed fairly to the advent of any given pipeline infrastructure project? Underscore *fairly*. How many emissions can be attributed solely to a project under consideration, which would not be generated otherwise by another heavy oil source or alternative transportation infrastructure, considering that no single project impacts global demand for heavy oil?

A proper determination — such as the assessments carried out by the U.S. Department of State for KXL and by Environment Canada for TMX — leaves the task of assessing net incremental emissions to the politicians; they must assess whether the emissions are material in the context of prevailing carbon policy, with due regard for the economic value hanging in the balance. The issue is not whether there will be incremental emissions, but rather whether they are material to Canadian energy and carbon policy. In the case of KXL, the Department of State explicitly deemed those emissions immaterial, and in the case of TMX, Environment Canada credibly analyzed fairly attributable emissions.[1] Ultimately, however, and this is especially true in light of Canada's Paris commitment, only the federal government can definitively decide on materiality. Can TMX and LNG Canada, for instance, be rationalized or not? Bill C-69 does not prescribe how to calculate incremental emissions, and does not provide any context for how the approval process would deal with the reality of incremental emissions. Rather, it leaves the regulatory process to explore the question without limit, presumably with the discretion to provide its own findings on materiality and consistency with national carbon and energy policy.

Little is to be gained from an approval process captured by those convinced that Canada cannot abide any incremental emissions from its hydrocarbon production, who cite Canada's commitment to a 25 percent reduction from current emissions by 2030 to argue that no incremental emissions from the hydrocarbon sector can ever be rationalized, especially when Canada has so few low-cost emissions reduction opportunities. This is the long-standing position of the Canadian ENGO community. Whatever this argument's merits as Canadian carbon policy, and as de facto Canadian energy policy, it should not be debated in the regulatory forum, but within the political process. The duly elected governments must be the entities to clarify whether the ENGOs' position in fact describes Canadian carbon policy.

All this raises the question: If Canadian ENGOs' absolutist position is not to define Canadian carbon policy, then what should? I set out my own view fully in the next chapter. The bottom line is that the government must clarify whether additional hydrocarbon production is consistent with Canadian carbon policy and, if it is, to define the standard of what constitutes acceptable additional emissions. As an example, the Notley government implemented an oil sands emissions cap of 100 MT annually — an increase of roughly 30 MT from existing levels. This government never, admittedly, set out how to implement such a cap, notwithstanding the task force it created to do just that. The Trudeau government has stated that the Alberta oil sands emissions cap helped it rationalize the approval of TMX, but it provided no plan to appropriate that standard, ignore it, or make it more stringent. This cap could have provided greater clarity for prospective proponents as an ultimate emissions limit.

As Bill C-69 stood in early 2019, the climate test added only more open-endedness and ambiguity to the approval process, more scope for procrastination, and ultimately it added obstruction. It would cause prospective proponents to avoid the entire approval process. After all, what inference would they make, watching each application become a de facto public symposium on Canadian carbon policy? No one would want to get wrapped up with a government so equivocal about additional hydrocarbon production that sanction may never occur, or may occur only under untenable conditions. Canada needs to remove the climate test from the regulatory process, full stop, and the federal government must provide clarity so that proponents can determine whether any given project may be possible in Canada at all.

Beyond the climate test, Bill C-69 adds further subjective tests to the approval process, such as the possible impact of a project on Indigenous groups' sustainability, and on gender considerations. As of the end of 2018, Bill C-69 remained silent on how such considerations would be applied, and on their materiality in the overall assessment. More ambiguity and risk. More opportunity to stretch out the approval process.

A further deficiency of Bill C-69 rests with its lack of standing tests and enforced timelines. CEAA 2012 was vilified for asserting more rigorous tests for parties seeking formal participant status in the hearings for energy projects; to achieve standing, parties had to show that the project stood to impact them directly. Instructively here, TMX and Northern Gateway were processed quite distinctly, TMX under CEAA 2012 and Northern Gateway under the original 1992 statute. The NEB panel for TMX applied greater rigour to applications for standing, in contrast with the expansive and distorting process applied to Northern Gateway, though not as stringently as the statute allowed. In the case of Northern Gateway, deliberate ENGO-led tactics stretched out the hearing process, but that was not the case for TMX. Enbridge's application for Northern Gateway was deemed complete in September 2010, and the NEB recommended approval in December 2013, close to three and half years later. Just the hearing continued for over a year and a half.

In contrast, the NEB recommended TMX's approval only twenty-four months after its application was deemed complete. The timing improvement arose not only from applying more rigorous standing tests but also from conducting interrogatories in written form rather than by cross-examination. The TMX process conformed to the statutory time constraints set out in CEAA 2012. Interestingly, in its August 2018 decision on TMX, the Federal Court of Appeal rejected claims against that NEB process. With whatever chaos that court decision caused, it at least validated CEAA 2012. In C-69, however, the Trudeau government eliminated the standing test altogether, granting standing to any individual or advocacy group, Canadian or otherwise, that wants it, regardless of direct impact, regardless of the probative value of any evidence provided, and regardless of any past record of regulatory obstruction. Furthermore, C-69 allows the minister of the environment to extend deadlines, but no one else: not the Cabinet or any other ministry with an obvious interest in the outcome and process of such approval processes.

CEAA 2012 was not, by any means, perfect. Its provisions on timing became binding only once an application was deemed complete. As the Energy East process demonstrated, obstructionists could stretch out and complicate that determination itself. But CEAA 2012 did constrain ministerial discretion on timing to some degree, and, with its standing test provisions, it attempted to restore the process's efficiency. Bill C-69 enables an empathetic government to extend the approval process unreasonably. Stretching out the regulatory process serves only those implacably opposed to development. To secure a fairer process that balances the interests of applicants with those of legitimate intervenors, the CEAA 2012 provisions on standing and statutory timeline should stay in place.

Bill C-69 would appoint regulatory panel members, executive officers, and other governance officials for criteria other than technical competence and experience — for other "values" and identity considerations. Again, the Trudeau government seemingly fails to understand what a regulatory process must achieve. It is not properly a discovery process, a focus group, or a polling exercise; rather, it is a technocratic exercise to set appropriate conditions on proposed projects — conditions that mitigate impacts and provide appropriate accommodations to impacted stakeholders, consistent with acceptable global standards and risk tolerances, ideally for projects already determined in the public interest. Appointing regulators on the basis of ethnicity and gender instead of competency and fairness is unjustifiable.

Under Bill C-69, the NEB has no role in the assessment and approval process. The bill reduces the board's function, in a rebranded entity, to overseeing operating facilities under federal jurisdiction. Project approvals fall to a new entity called the Impact Assessment Agency, which replicates the NEB's existing mandate to carry out its basic technocratic functions. This new entity is encumbered with a governance structure that adds little beyond providing certain interest groups with representation. The Trudeau government has vilified the NEB with its "lack of trust and confidence" meme, seemingly based primarily on the Northern Gateway recommendations. Both Trudeau and Butts personally opposed Northern Gateway, even before the NEB made its recommendation, which was supported by extensive analysis of the submitted evidence. However, they never laid out the deficiencies of that analysis.

More broadly, they made no case against the existing NEB's integrity or competency to carry out its mandate according to its own governing statute and CEAA 2012. A regulator can be deemed world-class based on its technical competence and demonstrated fairness, on its proven ability to carry out core functions efficiently, in a manner that provides predictable and robust decisions consistent with governing statutes — none of which has anything to do with identity, gender, or political affiliation. Who could suggest that the NEB has failed historically to meet this standard? Only those who resent that it refused to become complicit in obstructing key infrastructure. Despite all rhetoric to the contrary, "modernization" is not, truly, the issue. What real value is gained from deconstructing the NEB? None.

Finally, Bill C-69 leaves open the possibility that it may be applied to areas traditionally left to provincial jurisdiction. The hydrocarbon production industry wondered, particularly, if C-69 would extend to provincial production facilities, not only for major new oil sands project but in normal course extensions for existing operations. At the end of 2018, that ambiguity remained unresolved. Obviously, applying the C-69 climate test as extremely as the ENGO community insists would undo the development of all additional hydrocarbon at its source. Is this the Trudeau government's intent? If the Trudeau government expects Alberta to abide by the existing oil sands emissions cap in order to avoid extending C-69 to those emissions, it has not said so explicitly. If it does, then what will happen if that cap is reversed by a conservative government in Alberta? At present, what counts as a "designated project"? What projects fall under the jurisdiction of C-69 remains ambiguous, but they are not necessarily limited to traditional areas of federal jurisdiction.

Bill C-69 is not regulatory reform. It is an unbalanced and extreme attempt to placate those who have achieved rejections of major hydrocarbon infrastructure by obstructing the existing Canadian regulatory process. To restate the obvious, if C-69 does not work for private capital, it will ensure only that hydrocarbon development is frustrated. Instead of making an explicit commitment to future growth of Canadian hydrocarbon production, the Trudeau government has created a future regulatory process that will only frustrate it. Trudeau's own rhetoric is irreconcilable with the reality of C-69, and even outright delusional. In a November 2018 speech at the Calgary Chamber of Commerce, he stated:

> I think one of the best ways of reducing profits, reducing royalties, and reducing production on people's lands is to not get anything built, and we don't want to not get anything built. We want to actually move forward on a process that is going to get approval but also give clarity, give clear timelines and a predictable frame for international investors, for proponents of big projects. That's what people have been asking for. Now, on Bill C-69, we've been listening.

He added that "the previous government did minimize assessment and partnerships with Indigenous people, which doesn't work." But he did not mention that Northern Gateway was undone by his own unilateral, unjustified decision. Nor did he acknowledge that the morass of TMX resulted from his own government's failure to carry out final Crown consultation consistent with Supreme Court and Federal Court of Appeal expectations.[2] Trudeau's disingenuous performance in Calgary compelled many to question his basic policy position on hydrocarbon growth in Canada.

At of the end of 2018, the Trudeau government, meanwhile, had disclosed no material amendments to Bill C-69.

CHAPTER 9

Climate Policy for Canada —
to Unify or to Polarize?

IF CANADA IS EVER to find a national consensus on whether or not to accept a growing hydrocarbon industry, it must first agree on what would constitute a credible and proportionate climate policy. We stipulate at the outset that any incremental greenhouse gas emissions translate into a higher probability of higher global temperatures and in turn into more disruption of the physical environment; and, yes, completely decarbonizing our existing energy systems would contain the risk of climate change. The world needs to contain the risk of climate change, and that may represent an existential threat to the hydrocarbon-based industries and economies reliant on them. However, decarbonization will impose real costs on current economies. Ideally, the issue should be framed as one of risk management, seeking the optimal mix of policy to minimize the risk of extreme climate change effects within politically palatable economic costs. Restated in terms of pricing, the issue should be to seek a carbon price that reflects the net cost and benefit of climate change over time. That net cost should be imposed on the utilization of hydrocarbons, "the social cost of carbon." Obviously, this is an idealized policy response. Sadly, it is not the direction that the UN process has taken.

Canada has consistently participated in the UN's climate process since its inception in 1992. The country has embraced emissions reduction targets that conformed substantially to U.S. commitments, without regard for the relative cost of compliance. Even at the end of 2018, the Trudeau government insisted that it was still committed to its Paris emissions reduction targets. It has never transparently quantified the cost of compliance, however, implying instead that Canada would embark on a joyful, altruistic adventure, transitioning to a green economy and away from its economic dependence on hydrocarbon production. This is the same government that spent $4.5 billion to salvage TMX, and that sanctioned the domestic LNG Canada project — decisions that will both inevitably increase Canadian emissions.

Suffice it to say, the Trudeau government is conflicted between credible carbon policy and the economic contribution of hydrocarbons to the Canadian economy. My question here is whether Canada can establish an intellectually credible carbon policy that would reinforce national unity instead of further polarizing Canadians — a policy that would serve Canada's economic interests while assuming a proportionate contribution to dealing with climate risk, relative to what Canada's major trading partners are prepared to do. It remains my view that such a policy is possible. Political leadership needs to create a national consensus for carbon pricing, appropriately conditioned as the pre-eminent policy instrument, and that views reduction targets as aspirational, not binding, obligations. Underscore *aspirational*.

To review the facts that must inform policy design: Canada emits less than 2 percent of global carbon in absolute terms, but, as a function of its relatively small population, climate, geography, and industrial structure, we are a relatively high per capita emitter. In 2016 Canada emitted roughly 700 MT of carbon dioxide equivalent, which is roughly 100 MT higher than its 1990 emissions. The increase resulted mostly from economic growth within Canada, much of it from significant new oil sands production.[1] Of course, the distribution of emissions throughout Canada is not uniform; Alberta leads with over 250 MT, or 35 percent of national emissions, per year, and this one province's growth in emissions of roughly 100 MT per year since 1990 accounts for virtually all the national growth in that period. Ontario comes in second, with just over 150 MT per year.[2]

Unlike many of its major trading partners, Canada has already substantially decarbonized its electric generation sector, using nuclear generation in Ontario and New Brunswick, and hydro in Quebec, Manitoba, and British Columbia. This leaves the country with limited low-cost opportunities to reduce emissions further. The emissions reduction target that Canada tabled in late 2015 in Paris requires reducing emissions by roughly 200 to 500 MT per year. In 2009 and 2015 Canada set national carbon targets that conformed to the U.S. target — roughly a 25 percent reduction from 2005 levels. However, the two countries face entirely different costs of compliance. Canada would require carbon prices or equivalent policies of more than $200 per tonne, while the United States could come close simply by continuing to replace coal with gas and some renewables. This is a profound difference.

In 2018 the Pan-Canadian Framework on Clean Growth and Climate Change committed Canada to carbon pricing of $10 per tonne initially, rising to $50 per tonne by 2022. This was one of the world's most stringent pricing commitments, and certainly exceeded any within North America. Yet Canada has the capacity to expand both oil sands production and natural gas production for LNG. With sufficient pipeline capacity, annual oil sands production additional to existing production could exceed one million barrels per day by 2030, for a total approaching four million barrels per day. Each world-scale LNG facility developed in Canada would present an additional 4 to 5 billion cubic feet of natural gas per day of production when fully developed, compared to existing western Canadian gas production of roughly 16 billion cubic feet per day.[3] Such forecasts assume continued positive global economic growth, no extreme climate-driven policy interventions by major global economies, and geopolitical stability.

Obviously, the development of all of these resources would result in a substantial increase in Canada's greenhouse gas emissions, the source of climate change.

We need to remember the context of the UN process to address climate change, in which developed countries have accepted voluntary physical emissions reduction targets toward the ultimate ambition of limiting global temperature increase to 2 degrees Celsius, or better yet to 1.5 degrees. This process has never centred on carbon pricing, considering it as an adjunct, peripheral policy instrument at best, nor has it focused on finding consensus on an appropriate social cost of carbon that informs the stringency of carbon pricing; that is, on the net economic cost of rising temperature relative to its benefits, including the value of hydrocarbon consumption. For Canada, with its higher costs of compliance, the UN's approach to date, of emissions reduction commitments, has proved particularly problematic.

But even if the world does meet the Paris emissions reduction commitments, the world will come nowhere close to containing the temperature increase at 2 degrees Celsius, and will likely experience a global temperature increase in the range of 3.2 degrees. Meanwhile, current policies excluding the Paris pledges would likely result in a 3.4 degree increase, even though the UN still tries to brand the agreement as somehow consistent with containing global temperature increase within 1.5 to 2 degrees.[4] For the world to seriously embrace 1.5 degree containment as its target, some analysis suggests it would require between $1.6 trillion and $3.8 trillion in "energy system supply-side investments" between today and 2050, or, in more tangible terms, we would need to build the equivalent of one to two nuclear power plants every day until 2050, while shutting down thousands of coal, gas, and oil-fired power plants as well.[5] Containing 1.5 degrees would also require utilizing still unproven technologies to remove accumulated CO_2 from the atmosphere.

It should be noted that the International Panel on Climate Change's modelling process for predicting global temperature increase from rising atmospheric greenhouse gases is still contentious within some elements of the scientific community. Ideally, the UN process should have generated a more rational policy direction that stressed adaptation and transition, based on a global consensus on both carbon pricing and how to deploy the resulting revenue.

Whatever the numbers are, the fact is that Canada, on balance, would likely benefit economically from higher global temperature — warming would improve the country's agricultural output and reduce space heating demands, resulting in a negative social cost of carbon. This contention has been validated by researchers in California and Italy, who published their findings in *Nature*.[6] Anyone who has endured a Canadian winter might find this intuitively obvious, but we must also acknowledge that CO_2 impacts on global warming are global. A tonne of emitted CO_2 contributes equally to climate change regardless of where it comes from. Canada is of course culpable of creating social costs of carbon in other countries, but no more so than any other historic hydrocarbon consumer and producer.

All of this provides the necessary context for what a more rational, credible carbon policy for Canada would look like. This policy must be one that reinforces national unity rather than creating further alienation within western Canada, and without posing an unreasonable cost on Canada relative to costs that our major trading partners are prepared to impose on themselves. Canada has only one reasonable carbon policy instrument that can meet those conditions: a national carbon tax. Full stop. The tax should be applied at first in the range of the Notley government's carbon tax of $30 per tonne of carbon equivalent, but preferably specified in U.S. currency to keep the price straightforwardly comparable to other pricing regimes. On this tax, three key conditions apply.

First, the tax's stringency must be a function of equivalent taxes, direct or indirect, from countries that Canada trades with, weighted by volume of bilateral trade. Obviously, this implies that Canada would ultimately have to be highly aligned with U.S. carbon policy, at least in respect of carbon pricing, explicitly or implicitly. If, for instance, a post-Trump United States imposes on itself pricing that exceeds $100 per tonne, Canada will need to internalize that and determine an equivalent carbon tax level. Canada must accept the logical consequence of this condition: Canadian carbon pricing must be constrained to align with its key trading partners, primarily the United States.

Carbon pricing via a uniform, national tax would be Canada's only carbon policy instrument. Canada accepts whatever carbon emissions reductions arise from the additional price signal represented by the tax. Existing national targets, then, become aspirations rather than binding policy mandates. This logic is inescapable. If the world cannot price carbon at levels required to create the reductions sufficient to meet Paris commitments, why would Canada? We should impose on ourselves only the same cost of emitted carbon that the rest of the world's countries are prepared to impose on themselves. We must internalize the additional price signal from the carbon tax across our economy, and each Canadian must confront that price when deciding whether to generate an incremental emission or not. A country can specify a price or an emissions reduction quantity, but not both. For Canada, it must be a price.

Second, the government must strive to keep its carbon tax neutral for taxpayers, reducing income and corporate income taxes to compensate for the carbon tax, recognizing that the most regressive impacts of the national tax must be offset as much as possible and that some tax revenue should be allocated to adaptation investment. This strategy would minimize the carbon tax's negative impact on GDP. Canadian industries would require a rebate to ensure competitiveness when trading with countries without any carbon tax or with taxes substantially smaller than ours.

Third, Canada should have no other interventions, subsidies, mandates, or regulations, whether to deal with market failure or to accelerate physical emissions reductions. The national carbon tax should be the only policy instrument. The tax must be applicable uniformly across Canada on all emissions at their source.

The Trudeau government has not to date articulated the cost required to achieve its Paris emissions reduction targets, and certainly it has not, in simple, transparent terms, communicated the required carbon pricing. How high will Canadian carbon prices have to ascend from $50 per tonne in 2022 to meet Canada's Paris obligation? None of this vagueness is surprising, since credible analysis has always shown that carbon prices would likely have to exceed $200 per tonne to achieve that target.[7] The federal government disclosed one bar graph within its Pan-Canadian Framework document. The graph is more opaque than transparent, but it clearly suggests that Canada would require further significant interventions to meet its target.[8]

Minister of the Environment and Climate Change Catherine McKenna speaks in the House of Commons, January 2019.

To restate a key reality: Canada, with little coal left in the electric generation mix, does not have any large source of "cheap" emissions reductions. We would need to constrain hydrocarbon use domestically, or constrain hydrocarbon production processes that generate emissions, most obviously oil sands production and LNG production. It is one thing to ask oil sands and LNG facilities to internalize a carbon tax equal to what Canada's trading partners are imposing on themselves, but quite another to impose absolute prohibitions on hydrocarbon production. Essentially, such a policy would result in an infinite carbon price. And that is the key point — a Canadian carbon tax needs to be understood as the cost to emit carbon, full stop.

A Canadian government could ignore competitive issues and simply impose a $200 per tonne carbon tax to alter domestic energy consumption and hydrocarbon production for export. If some entities could afford the $200 per tonne tax, then presumably they could continue to consume hydrocarbons and to emit the associated carbon. Of course, it would be ridiculous for Canada to impose $200 per tonne when most of the world cannot come to terms with carbon pricing, explicitly or implicitly, much higher than $30 per tonne.

Some advocate that Canada can "afford" sufficient offshore "credits" or "offsets" to buy its Paris compliance. The price of these offsets, according to this logic, may cost less than the level of domestic carbon pricing required to physically achieve them within Canada. Offsets ostensibly occur when one country pays another to eliminate an emission. Of course, this presumes that the country with "low-cost" emissions reductions would not have eliminated the emission in any case, and was not compelled to eliminate that emission. Ignoring that rather significant inconsistency in the credibility of offsets, a country buying offsets would be able to achieve physical emissions reductions at lower cost than by reducing emissions physically within its own borders. This strategy would see Canada sending dollars out of the country to meet its national targets, even if that value were higher than the going carbon tax.

To date, the Trudeau government has not indicated a firm intention to acquire foreign offsets as the ultimate default to achieve compliance. Would the government be able to purchase such offsets at less than the going domestic carbon price? Can it acquire them at a value less than that required to comply with Paris through physical measures within Canada? The real question is why Canada would take on offsets when their costs could well exceed that of the applicable domestic carbon tax. The answer, of course, is that offsets make sense only for a Canada obsessed with physical compliance over internalizing the cost of emissions to the same degree as its major trading partners. And even if any Canadian government did resort to offsets, it would still need to clarify whether the going domestic carbon price, if paid, would allow Canadians and Canadian industry to continue to emit carbon.

The UN has never, in the history of its climate process, and especially in the negotiations leading up to the Paris Accord, been prepared to make carbon pricing its fundamental policy instrument. The Paris process devolved to each country voluntary national emissions reduction commitments, eschewing the alternative of uniform global carbon pricing as beyond the negotiation process's capacity to achieve collective agreement on. But a UN process centred on pricing rather than targets would have been less problematic for Canada in respect of compliance.

The Trump administration could have led the world to reinvent the entire Paris climate process, steering it away from emissions reduction targets and toward carbon pricing, through its first secretary of state, Rex Tillerson, a long-time ExxonMobil CEO. Tillerson was as conversant as any of the UN's political leadership, since its inception, with carbon policy alternatives and their economic implications, both domestically and internationally, and ExxonMobil had been a long-time advocate of carbon taxes as the appropriate carbon policy instrument. Trump could have made Tillerson accountable for dealing with the entire climate change file, but when he withheld that accountability, any chance of a climate-process reboot was lost. Bolstered by Trump's threat to withdraw from the entire Paris process, Tillerson might have convinced the UN climate panel to reconsider basic elements of its process. We will never know; instead, the Trump administration simply withdrew from the Paris agreement in June 2017. Ironically, despite Trump's withdrawal of the United States, and despite the absence of any federal climate policy from his administration, the United States continued, into 2018, to reduce carbon emissions in its electricity sector, a reduction that was driven mainly by market forces.[9] The advent of shale gas technology drove down natural gas pricing, and costs declined for solar and wind components.

The United States was able to drive down its emissions because of the existing composition of electrical generation infrastructure. The same conditions do not exist in Canada. It is important to appreciate that a significant component of what we count as Canadian emissions in fact result from export demand. The federal government analysis conducted in 2011 confirmed that our exported emissions exceed our imported ones,[10] an imbalance that must only have grown since then, as our energy export has largely taken the form of oil sands–derived product. LNG development, if it grows, will increase exported emissions as well. The point is that a substantial component of Canada's emissions load is driven by hydrocarbon consumption outside the country. If Canada does not supply the demanded hydrocarbons, another country will.

Nevertheless, Canada, as of the end of 2018, remains firmly committed to achieving its Paris targets, exemplified by McKenna's *cri de coeur*, "I'm no quitter," shortly after Canadian ENGO leaders called for her to resign over inadequate progress toward those targets plus continued support for oil sands pipeline infrastructure and LNG development.[11] Still, neither she nor they transparently indicated to Canadians what compliance would cost in absolute or relative terms.

We must assess the current state of Canadian politics, and ask if it has the capacity to embrace these principles of a more rational carbon policy, as I have outlined above. The simple answer, alas, seems to be no.

Consider Canada's conservative politicians, federal and provincial. Incredibly, virtually all of them, perhaps with the exception of Manitoba premier Brian Pallister, adamantly oppose carbon pricing, especially in the form of carbon taxes. Virtually all of the country's current conservative leaders, from the premier of Ontario to the premier of Alberta, have promised an alternative to carbon taxes without tabling any specifics. They are all too likely to replicate Harper's prospective sectoral regulations, and will likely offer more in the way of promises than implementation. They provide no clarity on the relative cost of regulation versus carbon taxes, invoking vague technology breakthroughs and unspecified regulations, presumably less costly than a transparent carbon price. Their historic failure to implement credible carbon policy has only diminished their political credibility and the chance of finding a genuine national consensus. They eschew climate denialism publicly, but the net result of their rhetoric and inaction results in diminished credibility.

Harper left a genuinely counterproductive legacy, one that blights the right's progress toward a national consensus on carbon pricing via transparent, uniform, national carbon taxes. I concede that one should be skeptical of promises that a government has the ability to enforce the revenue neutrality of any carbon tax regime. Any tax, once implemented, may become additive to overall tax collection. That is a concern, but it does not delegitimize carbon taxes, especially in the Canadian context. What alternative achieves climate policy credibility at less cost than carbon taxes, conditioned on the terms I have set out above?

Canadian conservatives (of whichever party) cannot even move to a point of setting out conditions for acceding to carbon pricing — conditions that would allow the construction and operation of KXL or TMX, or force the Liberals to stand down on Bill C-69. It is dispiriting that much of this position is grounded in mere populist politics; voters disgruntled and alienated from the preoccupations of national elites demand that there be no carbon tax, and the conservative leaders comply. Worst of all, by rigidly rejecting the only logical policy instrument for this country, our conservative politicians actually hurt the long-term strategic interests of Canada, specifically preventing the country from fully seizing the economic contribution from its hydrocarbon resource.

A majority of Canadians may support pipelines and the economic contribution of hydrocarbons to the national economy, but that same majority expects credible carbon policy, notwithstanding that few are eager to pay for that policy themselves.[12] Rachel Notley's 2015 climate plan got one point, maybe the most important point, right, and that was carbon pricing. The plan did apply unneeded interventions to the electric market and oil sands emissions, and it failed to embrace revenue neutrality, but carbon pricing remained its most important element. Carbon pricing was the element that legitimized Alberta climate policy, though the Alberta and federal right never conceded as much.

And the Canadian left? The federal NDP, the Green Party's various manifestations, the major Canadian ENGOs, and their prominent individual propagandists — David Suzuki, Naomi Klein, and Tzeporah Berman, for instance — all expect Canada to not only meet its Paris emissions reduction obligations, regardless of cost, but also to rapturously embrace decarbonization as a moral imperative. Needless to say, none of these groups or individuals have been held to account for the economic contraction they would impose on Canada, in a world with enduring demand for Canadian hydrocarbons and as yet no evidence of collective action to even approach decarbonization.

For Canada, that means no hydrocarbon development, full stop. And the left will use any obstruction levers available to make that happen: for them, the moral imperative of decarbonization, to avoid a world of 3 degrees Celsius temperature increase, is fundamental. None of these players apply conditionality to a Canada committed to decarbonization, even if the world comes nowhere close to the interventions required to achieve it. None concede that Canada must follow, not lead, the world's developed countries on climate policy. None advocate for conditioned carbon pricing, as outlined earlier in this chapter, for focusing the national debate on the allocation of the tax collection, from strict revenue neutrality to adaptation investment.[13]

Contrast the Canadian left with the evolution of the Notley government, which appreciated that preserving Alberta's economy could only be rationalized by establishing credible carbon policy. It did not, however, foresee the resistance to market access for Alberta's oil sands product. Notley's government recognized the basic fiscal arithmetic: Alberta's fiscal situation would deteriorate, without that breakthrough on market access, as has been evidenced by the massive discounts on Canadian oil sands production in late 2018, and the growing public debt over the course of the Notley tenure as Premier.

And then the Liberals. We might have expected them to perform their historic function of reinforcing national unity by finding an appropriate balance between enforcing national interests and accommodating those alienated within the country. Doubtless, key figures in the Trudeau government believed that was what they were trying to do. In the end, though, it seems that keeping Quebec within Confederation for the sake of national unity is one thing, but relating fairly to Alberta has been more problematic. Pierre Elliott Trudeau fought with Alberta about how the economic rents from hydrocarbon production ought to be shared, and on the degree of federal control of the Canadian hydrocarbon industry; but despite the alienation that fight spawned in Alberta, the federal government never questioned the fundamental value of hydrocarbon production to Canada. Of course, Justin Trudeau presides over more complicated circumstances, in which climate change risk puts into question the future contribution of hydrocarbons to the Canadian economy.

As I stated earlier, the Trudeau government seems willing to abide TMX, LNG Canada, and KXL, but nothing more — "abide" being the operative word. Some may observe that spending $4.5 billion on TMX represents a lot of "abiding," but the government's actions since the August 31 Federal Court of Appeal decision left the project's outcome to play out in 2019. Bill C-69, as is, leads to the entirely logical inference that the Liberals have no interest in expanded hydrocarbon growth within Canada. So, it must be concluded, the Liberal government's basic sympathies doubtless lie with those who deem dealing with the climate change risk a moral imperative, and who profess that decarbonizing can lead to a more sustainable, more authentic low-carbon economy without substantial economic loss.

The Trudeau Liberals, relative to Canadian conservatives, have, I concede, embraced carbon pricing as a significant component of Canadian carbon policy; but taken on its face, the Pan-Canadian Framework promises further interventions beyond carbon pricing to ensure Canada meets its Paris commitments, interventions whose costs may far exceed the going carbon tax value. Does the payment of a carbon tax confer on the individual or entity paying the tax the right to emit, or doesn't it?

The problem is that the Trudeau government appears incapable of accepting the three elements necessary for a more rational carbon policy for Canada: carbon pricing via a national tax as the pre-eminent, if not sole, policy instrument for dealing with the climate change risk within Canada; constrained carbon-price stringency, according to what Canada's major trading partners are prepared to impose on themselves; and an acknowledgement that the existing Paris commitments are aspirational rather than binding. A uniform carbon tax provides the requisite market signal, not direct interventions into the economy. The second simply accepts reality — Canada is not going to lead the world on climate change. The third is just a matter of logic — climate policy can either specify the price for emitted carbon or it can dictate how much carbon may be emitted in aggregate, and by what allocation method. Accepting these conditions would require an economic maturity and literacy that seems beyond this government, which gives key political and bureaucratic appointments to individuals with life experience divorced from the processes of wealth creation and preservation within Canada.

Under continued Trudeau governments, Canada will have a national carbon tax, regardless of whether certain provinces choose not to impose an equivalent tax. But the Trudeau government has never said that carbon pricing is equivalent to the right to emit carbon or that its future stringency has some limit based on what Canada's major trading partners are imposing on themselves.

Doubtless a Trudeau government would welcome the 2020 restoration of a Democratic administration in the United States, and a renewed U.S. commitment to the Paris Climate Accord. Such an administration would almost certainly restore an activist climate policy on carbon pricing and other market interventions, especially within transportation and electric generation. From all of this, the Trudeau government would surely take solace, especially if the United States implemented some form of national carbon pricing. Of course, the United States has a distinct advantage — it has been able to increase its hydrocarbon production in both oil and gas over the past decade while physically reducing emissions, simply by reducing coal in its electric generation sector. Canada may remain a growing physical emitter well into the next decade, especially if it builds the pipelines and LNG facilities currently on the table. If the American people re-elect Trump, however, the Trudeau government will become increasingly unsettled, if not even more incoherent, trying to align with the reality of Trumpian non-carbon policy, while trying to preserve Canadian competitiveness.

The Liberals offer incoherence and opacity on carbon policy rather than a set of robust principles that emphasize realism, self-interest, and market mechanisms. But, to their credit, they are prepared to accept carbon pricing, an inescapable element for any credible and proportionate carbon policy for Canada. Still, simply supporting carbon pricing conceptually is not enough. It must be justified to Canadians as the only option that can ever provide carbon policy credibility and potentially still enable a growing hydrocarbon sector at the same time. It is not an option for Canada to have no carbon policy, but we must accept carbon policy as a matter of internalizing the climate risk economically, at a level no higher than Canada's major trading partners are prepared to impose on themselves.

The global climate change risk is the ultimate "tragedy of the commons" — only collective action can avoid a suboptimal outcome, and without collective action each country has too much incentive to "free ride." Canada, however, faces pressure from without and within to do more than any other country, and so we face becoming the inverse of the free rider — the altruistic doofus.

Some may view what I propose for Canadian carbon policy as nothing more than sophistry. Some will say that I draw erroneous moral equivalence between pricing and reducing or avoiding physical emissions. My response is that Canada does have the option to sacrifice its hydrocarbon production industry by denying its market access demands and gradually contracting its export-related production. But would it make any material difference to global emission levels? Would such a sacrifice make any economic sense in the real world that Canada finds itself in?

The entire IPCC/UNCCC (Intergovernmental Panel on Climate Change/United Nations Framework Convention on Climate Change) construct requires containing the growth of atmospheric concentrations of greenhouse gases, principally CO_2, to avert a potentially untenable global temperature increase of 2 degrees Celsius, or, ideally, 1.5 degrees; but to meet this goal, the world's major economies would have to collectively embrace decarbonization, completely eliminating hydrocarbons from the energy mix. Leaving aside the costs and benefits of a global commitment to decarbonization, and leaving aside also the uncertainties and limitations of the climate models, it is far from clear how and when to allocate emissions reductions and energy system conversion throughout the world, and the reality is that some countries have cheaper available emissions reduction possibilities than others. Those that still have coal to remove from their electricity fuel fix have cheaper available emissions reductions compared to countries that have already done that by means of hydro, nuclear, or renewables. The next available emissions reductions would have to come from the transportation sector and heating sector, at far higher costs than that of substituting natural gas for coal. How quickly can the world convert to all-electric vehicles? Or develop viable low-carbon air transport fuel substitutes? How much additional cost will the world take on to use electricity rather than hydrocarbons for space heating? Or for various industrial purposes? And when, if ever, will fundamental breakthroughs in electric storage technology be developed at a scale that would deal with the intermittency of wind and solar electricity generation?

Regardless of the UN or the IPCC or the ENGO movement, the world continues persistently to consume hydrocarbons, and countries that stand to produce those resources face a dilemma. How many would walk away from the real economic value at stake, when halting production in their own country alone would make little to no difference to world crude, natural gas, or coal demand, with some other country taking up the market share given up by Canada? Would the United States, even with a leftist Democrat as president, apply such policy to its own country, all in the name of dealing with the global risk of climate change?

In a world where hydrocarbon consumption is unlikely to be materially reduced over the next twenty to thirty years, but an enduring collective aspiration to deal with climate change persists, what is a credible moral and economic response for Canada? The point of a Canadian carbon tax is not so much the actual emissions reductions that arise from it, but rather the fundamental commitment to follow the world if it actually has the will to impose carbon prices on itself that would even begin to approach the levels required to achieve 2 degrees Celsius containment. The Canadian economy should internalize that price and let it adjust to that additional price signal. Full stop. And if the world, especially Canada's major trading partners, have will to impose on itself a carbon price of $200 per tonne, then Canada will follow. If the world can't take on such a price, Canada has no reason to do so either.

Canada cannot embrace carbon change denialism, but it would be as insane to embrace such carbon altruism that our economy is materially diminished. Canada can't be a free rider in dealing with climate change, but neither should we be the converse — a country that diminishes itself economically, and for no payoff, by sacrificing its hydrocarbon industry. Canadian politicians who advocate regulation or mandates to effect actual emissions reductions need to ask themselves whether the cost of those regulations exceeds the prevailing carbon price via the carbon tax. If they do, why impose them? Why insist on emissions reductions costlier than the value to our major trading partners of emitted carbon? There is no justification for it. Emissions reductions will occur consistent with the level of the carbon tax or expectations on the future level of that tax. Those are the emissions reductions that Canada should expect, and that is what the world should expect of Canada. If Canada's hydrocarbon industry can afford the carbon tax, albeit with appropriate import and export adjustments, then it should go forward, and Canadians and trading partners should not expect that industry to take on additional carbon emissions reductions. And that includes the required infrastructure — in a word, pipelines.

CHAPTER 10

An Inconvenient Reality

AN UNTENABLE RISK for any future major development of resources or related infrastructure must be confronted. Do the Indigenous Peoples of Canada currently possess a de facto veto or not on major infrastructure projects in Canada? At the end of 2018 this issue remained unresolved, and it may yet undo TMX, despite the Trudeau government's efforts to remedy the consultation deficiencies cited by the Federal Court of Appeal.

Not unlike the endlessly debated second amendment to the Constitution of the United States (the right to bear arms), Section 35 of the Canadian Charter of Rights and Freedoms is deceptively simple:

1. The existing aboriginal and treaty rights of the aboriginal people in Canada are hereby recognized and affirmed.
2. In this Act, "Aboriginal Peoples of Canada" includes the Indian, Inuit, and Métis Peoples of Canada.
3. For greater certainty, in subsection (1), "treaty rights" includes rights that now exist by way of land claims agreements or may be so acquired.[1]

What Section 35 means in practical terms has been defined since 1982 by the decisions of Canada's courts. Over that same period, the

Canadian Parliament has not clarified this language. Court decisions created, most notably, the Crown duty to consult, the federal fiduciary obligation to Indigenous Peoples, and decisions prescribing on what terms Aboriginal title can be infringed. The courts have been especially prescriptive in their interpretation of the "duty to consult," conflating that phrase with an expectation that industry proponents and governments engage with Indigenous Peoples to the point of accommodating critical deficiencies through adequate consultation. As importantly, the courts have established a standard by which Aboriginal title, or even the claim to such title, can justifiably be infringed, that is, when land can be used for certain purposes where a consensual agreement between proponents and First Nations does not exist for that use.

According to the Supreme Court ruling in *Tsilhqot'in Nation v. British Columbia* (2014), for the Crown to override Aboriginal title in the public interest it must have done the following:

1. The Crown must have carried out consultation and accommodation.
2. The Crown's actions must have been supported by a compelling and substantial objective.
3. The Crown's action must have been consistent with its fiduciary obligation to the Aboriginal body in question.[2]

The proponent must provide compensation for this infringement, akin to the compensation it must provide to any Canadian landowner whose land is expropriated for a project deemed in the public interest. But of course, in actual cases where the project proponents fail to obtain consensual agreement from Indigenous groups, these cases end up in the courts, which decide after the fact whether the proponent has consulted adequately, whether infringement is justified, and whether the proponent has proposed adequate compensation. These decisions are made in the courts long after the regulatory boards have recommended approval and those recommendations have achieved political sanction.

The Government of Canada has two options here. It can leave every future project to deal with claims of unjustified infringement, and allow accumulated case law to eventually establish some practical standard — with the expectation that any project development without complete unanimous consensual alignment from all affected Indigenous groups will face after-the-fact litigation — or it can attempt to create objective legislative standards on what constitutes sufficient consultation and justifiable infringement.

Consider if at some point in 2019, after the Trudeau government engages in further consultation as prescribed in the August 31 Federal Court of Appeal decision regarding TMX, that process culminates in a second approval from the federal government. Presumably, the government will have determined that adequate consultation has occurred, along with the requisite "grappling," to use the Federal Court of Appeal's word, and that the government has offered sufficient compensation or project adjustments to First Nations proximate to TMX, whether they explicitly agree or not. If certain First Nations remain unwilling to accede to the approval they will certainly move on to the courts yet again, with claims of unjustified infringement and endless injunctions in the interim, until, presumably, the highest courts in Canada rule on those claims. All the while, the project could remain frustrated if courts provide injunctions while adjudicating the entire case — a case that renders the preceding regulatory process pointless since it failed to accede to the unaccommodated demands of the implacably opposed.

If Canadian courts do ultimately validate the determinations of the Canadian regulatory process sanctioned by democratically elected governments, how long will it take to get to that point? How many months or years? And if the courts do not provide that ruling on TMX, what is Canada left with? A suspended project? A project built but not yet allowed to operate until such litigation is resolved? Or a project built and operating but subsequently suspended?

The fate of TMX is not hypothetical, and we cannot dismiss the potential for further litigation, even if the Trudeau government at some point in 2019 reapproves the project. As 2018 closed, no one could predict precisely how TMX would play out, or whether we would see the matter resolved in 2019 before the October federal election. But once approved, the project may face this litigation. Even as Alberta suffered under discounts driven by inadequate pipeline capacity, deficits increased, and unemployment abounded, the outcome was far from certain. As I write, one thing is clear: private capital can no longer abide this risk of endless after-the-fact litigation, as if it ever could. Meanwhile, those who seek to disable all hydrocarbon growth and related infrastructure for whatever reason find obvious synergy with certain First Nations unwilling to make any accommodation with such projects and prepared to assert their rights, such as they are, to the extreme.

The saddest irony is that the vast majority of First Nations have come to consensual agreements on both TMX and LNG Canada. Call it consultation; call it accommodation: it was a fundamental part of the business-development process. These two projects have not yet achieved consensual agreements with certain coastal First Nations proximate to the project. Whatever regulatory process Canada uses for future federal approvals, after-the-fact litigation from First Nations at odds with projects that achieve approval remains an untenable risk. Parliament must clarify, and legislate, that the approvals of Canadian regulators sanctioned by elected members of parliament represent justified infringement. This is a reasonable expectation, regardless of whether such law is subsequently tested in the courts. But Canadians should expect the highest courts in Canada to interpret the law in the broadest context possible when adjudicating constitutional questions that go to the heart of what it means to be a Canadian, and all Canadians should receive equal treatment under the law. Additionally, the Canadian government should legislate objective standards of what constitutes adequate consultation, all in the context that Indigenous groups do not have a veto on project development.

Now, some may expect or demand that project developers simply concede that they require the consent of all concerned First Nations, regardless of a project's quality, economic value, and impact (including the extent to which it can be mitigated). In that case, one implacable Indigenous group could undo a project regardless of the consequences to the rest of the country, including other Indigenous groups. If we take this reasoning to its logical conclusion, then Aboriginal title becomes absolute, so that an Indigenous group requires no rationale or explanation for shutting down a project. Other commentators argue that the federal government, rather than legislating, should negotiate with Indigenous groups to define the extent of their jurisdiction over their own land, regardless of how long that process might take to complete, and regardless of what value must be lost in the interim.

We should remain duly skeptical that any future parliament will clarify this visceral and very real back-end risk. TMX will play out against it, as may yet LNG Canada. Going forward, the risk is untenable. Can the Canadian polity recognize the situation for what it is, and seriously set out to fix it?

CHAPTER 11

Breakdown

AT THE END OF 2018, Canada was in genuine breakdown. If that is not evident from the preceding chapters of this book, objective corroboration comes in the form of a national poll by the Angus Reid Institute, released early in 2019. It indicated that over 60 percent of Canadians conceded a "crisis" due to "a lack of new pipeline capacity" in Canada. Predictably, close to 90 percent of Albertans polled agreed with the use of the term "crisis," while, at the low end, only 40 percent of Quebecers did, with 61 percent in Ontario, Manitoba, and the Atlantic provinces. Saskatchewan polled at 74 percent, and British Columbia had a slight edge toward "crisis" with 53 percent.[1]

These results could be viewed positively by Albertans: all of the dysfunctions of the last ten years were not lost on a majority of Canadians. But will that public sentiment make any difference ultimately to politicians or the courts? Even if Canada is so fortunate to come through 2019 with certain infrastructure projects under construction, the fundamentals of that breakdown will still persist going forward — unless the change I have laid out in the three previous chapters is realized.

Canada has lost its capacity to reasonably seize economic opportunity, and is failing to understand that economic value validated by market forces comprises the only enduring means to grow national wealth, improve personal opportunity, and ultimately provide the capacity to sustain its social welfare programs. The obstruction and indifference applied against Alberta's hydrocarbons for the previous ten years, the subject of this book, are currently the prime example of this breakdown, but the same dynamic can and will be applied against other development projects. No one should have delusions to the contrary. The animus toward Alberta's hydrocarbons may be unique, but the contempt and mistrust for private capital to advance major development projects are not.

Canada and Alberta may pull through in 2019 by the skin of their teeth: we may see KXL and TMX under construction, the Enbridge Line 3 expansion near completion, and construction of a world-class LNG project underway in British Columbia without any significant outstanding litigation or physical disruption. If this does occur, it will not be because we have found a genuine national consensus or implemented necessary policy clarifications, but rather in spite of ourselves. That additional pipeline capacity would likely accommodate reasonable projections of oil sands growth out to the end of the next decade, and emerging Asian LNG markets may reinvigorate the Canadian natural gas market. An uneasy quid pro quo may hang together: the Trudeau government accommodates Alberta sufficiently on market access, and Alberta sustains enlightened carbon policy, even after Notley. But the likelihood of all four projects prevailing remains uncertain. Perhaps even highly uncertain.

In the interim, Alberta must deal with its economic circumstances on its own. That became starkly evident when the Notley government announced its decision late in 2018 to curtail aggregate oil production to improve short-term cash flow to both the oil sands production sector and its own treasury. The Trudeau government remained fundamentally indifferent, despite its feeble attempts at commiseration and inconsequential provisions of debt financing. Albertans know that ten years of market access frustration are responsible for their province's current economic circumstances, though the Trudeau government did not acknowledge that, and certainly took no responsibility for its culpability in substantially creating that outcome.

TMX is the only remaining market access alternative in the hands of the Canadian federal government; the others will be decided by American courts, regulatory entities, and politicians. Since the Federal Court of Appeal's August 31, 2018, decision on TMX, the Trudeau government has committed itself to remedying the cited deficiencies. But will it be able ultimately to rationalize a second approval in the context of preserving its "climate credibility," and in the face of inevitable confrontation from those First Nations that will never acquiesce to TMX? Alberta's future rests largely on these decisions, which will be made in the first half of 2019. If these projects do not get to construction in 2019, Canada's hydrocarbon production industry will atrophy, and Alberta will change fundamentally. Imagine Manitoba with mountains.

Alberta has developed an overwhelming sense of alienation and frustration. Albertans are the owners of hydrocarbon resources with substantial enduring value, in a world that has yet to show that it can consume materially fewer hydrocarbons than it does now, especially crude oil and natural gas, or that sustained global economic growth can be realized without continued hydrocarbon consumption. Rather than finding the collective will to effect the fundamental changes in energy systems required even to approximate containing warming to 2 degrees Celsius, the world will more likely have to adapt to a 3 degree global temperature increase. But for all that, the infrastructure required to get Alberta's hydrocarbon resources to market has been frustrated for the last ten years — frustrated primarily by the relentless efforts of an implacable environmental movement, irresponsible in its lack of regard for the economic consequences that would ensue from its agenda. Albertans also face at best an equivocal, and possibly hostile, Trudeau government that holds the fate of TMX in its hands, even as it remains staunchly committed to enacting legislation, specifically Bill C-69, that will likely disable any future growth in required hydrocarbon infrastructure, if not hydrocarbon production itself. Why wouldn't Albertans be deeply skeptical of the federal government's capacity ultimately to approve TMX a second time?

Alberta has long had to live with a national wealth transfer system that requires it to contribute substantial portions of its tax collections, generated by Albertans, to other provinces to help sustain their social welfare systems — some of which have been largely hostile or indifferent to Alberta's demands for market access.

Its interests seem to be at odds with a federal judiciary concerned with creating specific rights and obligations out of Section 35 of the Constitution. Meanwhile, that judiciary ignores broader considerations of the national interest, as a result creating uncertainty and ambiguity, especially in respect of having apparent regulatory approvals undone for alleged process deficiencies long after the fact.

Alberta must also contend with a national media and academic and financial elites who identify with, or are intimidated by, the most unproductive elements of the Canadian polity, those typified by their demands to "keep it in the ground," regardless of the cost to the country, rather than recognizing and embracing the economic contribution of hydrocarbon production to Canada. Even when reasonable politicians enact "progressive" climate policy, exemplified by the Notley climate plan, nothing tangible in return has been received, not in the form of market access, and certainly not in the form of unequivocal commitment to hydrocarbon production growth in Canada. Alberta has endured successive federal governments committed to implausible national carbon emissions reduction targets, with compliance costs for Canada far higher than what the country's major trading partners are prepared to impose on themselves. These targets, if taken as an inviolate binding national obligation, could lead to constraining Canada's hydrocarbon production, let alone denying any additional market access.

Does Canada work for Alberta anymore? Albertans ask this question more and more, and justifiably so. The province remains viscerally at odds with the centre-left mindset of those currently running the federal government, and likely with a majority of the Canadian polity as well.

Has Canada ever really worked for Alberta? Over my own lifetime — roughly the same period during which hydrocarbons were discovered and developed here, the early 1950s to the present — Alberta has enjoyed relatively high wealth thanks substantially to the constitutional provision to leave hydrocarbon ownership with the province. Albertans themselves built on that opportunity and natural endowment, remaining open to development and foreign capital while applying reasonable regulations and taxation. Alberta has of course faced historically hostile federal governments that would revisit how to share economic rent derived from hydrocarbon production. That, however, is not the issue in play at the moment. Today Alberta faces the existential question: Will the rest of Canada abide hydrocarbon production at all?

In the earlier chapters of Part Two I laid out how Canada's regulatory approval process, regime, and climate policy must change to restore functionality and coherence if Canada, and especially Alberta, is to develop its hydrocarbon resources into the future while also credibly contributing to dealing with the global climate change risk. All of that is for the future. Such changes may be beyond the capacity of the Canadian political process ever to deliver. In the short run, however, it comes down to whether these remaining market access projects can actually be built. If no pipelines begin construction in 2019, if LNG encounters obstruction either in the courts or on right of way, and if Alberta continues to receive deep discounts for its crude oil production, how extreme will the political reaction in this province become?

By the close of 2018, even as Alberta stolidly endured the frustration of market access, no prominent provincial politician publicly voiced that most visceral question: "Does Canada work for Alberta anymore?" Instead, Premier Notley encouraged Albertans to keep faith in the federal government to "do the right thing." Other Alberta politicians indulge in policy positions and rhetoric that will only make it more difficult for the Trudeau government to ultimately rationalize a second approval of TMX. But the inescapable reality is that the pipeline's fate lies in that government's hands.

American legal decisions may move KXL to construction early in 2019, reducing pressure on the Trudeau government to once again approve TMX. Between KXL and Enbridge Line 3, Alberta would have sufficient capacity for much of the next decade, albeit with no West Coast access. Procrastination may then become the default of the Trudeau government. But if those projects do not get to construction in 2019, a decision on TMX by midyear is virtually impossible for the Trudeau government to avoid. For TMX to proceed in 2019, Trudeau will have to determine that sufficient additional consultation and accommodation efforts have occurred, even if consensual agreement with certain First Nations has not been achieved, and that sufficient additional conditions on tankers related to the project have been applied. To provide such an approval would mean confronting the Canadian environmental movement and the B.C. First Nations that oppose the project, along with parts of Trudeau's political base that value redistribution of wealth and reconciliation over national economic self-interest, and that want to see Canada define its future without the economic contribution of its hydrocarbon resource. Even following a second approval, the project may likely confront another round of litigation. At that point, the federal government would face a defining decision: whether to invoke its full powers to ensure construction regardless of where efforts to gain injunctive relief may stand. Much the same remains in play for LNG Canada as well — will the government enforce Shell's right, and that of its pipeline partner, TransCanada, to build?

Trudeau et al. have to decide if they are willing to make the necessary decisions to seize economic growth when the opportunity presents itself — an opportunity validated not only by the private sector, but by the national regulatory process. Do they recognize that the economic contribution of Canadian hydrocarbons cannot be easily replicated? Or do they really believe that Canada can do without Alberta and its hydrocarbons, as a matter of economics, if not morality? Those who think so might consider the additional electrical generation and associated transmission lines that this decarbonized Canada would require. Will building this infrastructure prove any easier than building pipelines carrying oil sands–derived crude oil, especially if it involves substantial growth in nuclear power generation? Will the same institutional failures that have so beset Alberta's hydrocarbons also constrain this future? Of course they will.

But some lessons can only be learned in the hardest of ways, sometimes more than once. Canada has a government unreasonably skeptical of private sector energy investment decisions, especially related to hydrocarbons. It is a government that would alter a regulatory approval process that is based on setting appropriate conditions, mitigations, and accommodations for projects manifestly in the public interest, and instead would offer an open-ended discovery exercise based on subjective standards unclarified by the government itself. The Trudeau Liberals tolerate a regulatory process too vulnerable to undoing after the fact by courts without technical expertise or sufficient regard for the national interest. This reality will apply not only to hydrocarbons or to Bill C-69 or to Alberta. It transcends all that.

Is it Canada's future to fail to seize available economic opportunity due to the obstructions of those implacably opposed to development, those who demand unjustifiable and disproportionate economic rents and vetoes, and with the acquiescence of other Canadian institutions?

Trudeau has spoken consistently during his time as Liberal leader and prime minister about finding a balance between the environment and the economy, searching out illusory common ground between hydrocarbon potential and climate commitments as well as other environmental and social considerations. Perhaps he believes that he has tried to do just that. But the only rationalization of Bill C-69 relies on the naïve notion that any alienated party, if invited to participate in the approval process, will ultimately choose to support or at least acquiesce in projects under consideration. Trudeau appears to believe that enough consultation and process will eventually assuage the opponents, that broad consensus will emerge for any "good" project.

But no amount of process will alter the resolve of some opponents, whose opposition is implacable. That includes ENGOs that reject any additional impact on certain cumulative effects, and especially in respect of climate change; certain First Nations; and certain communities that reject any proximate development out of pure NIMBYism, regardless of whatever reasonable mitigation has been provided. Such groups expect a de facto veto on hydrocarbon development, and with that veto they plan to bring all such development to a halt. This is a reality that no amount of "process" can overcome.

Trudeau frivolously rejected Northern Gateway, "processed" Energy East out of existence, failed to accommodate Petronas LNG constructively, and has remained resolutely committed to the poison pill of Bill C-69. Trudeau's "balance" is now reduced to two projects on the hydrocarbon side of the scale: TMX and LNG Canada. He has explicitly approved these projects, but they cannot go forward unless he reapproves TMX and enforces the LNG Canada approval. Finding balance has proved much more difficult than Trudeau could have imagined, and the decisions required of him in 2019 on TMX, LNG Canada, and Bill C-69 run counter to how he surely wishes to be remembered — as an enlightened progressive who fundamentally changed Canada into a country that genuinely embraced dealing with climate change and tangibly advanced reconciliation, whatever that might mean precisely, and regardless of the costs.

If Trudeau ensures the construction and operations of these projects, carbon emissions will increase in Canada, making the country's Paris targets even less plausible than they already are. Moreover, if he imposes these projects on First Nations that remain implacably opposed to them, that will be a defining action of his tenure as prime minister. If he blinks and disables those projects, however, he will create de facto vetoes for the ENGOs and First Nations, and will not only alienate Alberta, but will sacrifice its economic future. Sacrificing Alberta may not represent a huge political cost in the short run — specifically in terms of the next federal election — but the country will be unalterably damaged. As Brexit in the United Kingdom and Donald Trump's election on the United States have shown, economic, social, and cultural polarization will find outlets for expression one way or another, changing the structure of nation states, perhaps permanently. Trudeau will preside over an ever more polarized country, hurtling toward a crisis of national unity.

Rachel Notley tried, on behalf of Albertans, to meet Ottawa with common ground and accommodation, primarily through climate policy. Carbon pricing via a transparent carbon tax, appropriately conditioned, remains the correct policy instrument for Alberta's circumstances, but enlightened climate policy without a concurrent breakthrough on market access is untenable for Alberta.

Trudeau has failed to confront the ENGO community with the premise that Canada must constrain its approach to climate change by imposing on itself costs no greater than what its major trading partners are prepared to impose on themselves. He has failed to confront implacably opposed First Nations with the premise that projects determined to be in the public interest must go forward. And he has failed to confront those who would ignore the historic and potential economic contribution from Alberta to the rest of Canada. But Trudeau is prime minister and may remain so into the next decade. For all his deficiencies, he did spend $4.5 billion to preserve a TMX option. But will he ultimately provide a second TMX approval? Uncertain. Then again, Trudeau may judge that the political costs of imposing TMX are too great, and decide that endless procrastination is preferable, relying on the belief that Alberta will accept frustrated market access and the slow, inexorable atrophy of its economy. Trudeau may hold to the view that Alberta could never find the will to separate from Canada, and that it has few alternatives to create leverage with the federal government. If separation is unthinkable, then Alberta is left to expect, or to hope, that Trudeau will do the right thing. That truly is the bottom line.

Alberta elites know that 2019 is not the same as 1980. The current confrontation is truly "existential." Will Alberta's hydrocarbon-based economy be allowed to grow, or won't it? Will Canada sacrifice its hydrocarbon industry for the sake of "outperforming" expectations on its contribution to containing the risk of global climate change, and to avoid future confrontations with First Nations? Canada ultimately accepted Alberta's demand for market price for its resources in the 1980s, albeit grudgingly; it took a new Conservative federal government to entrench the principle of market pricing for Canadian hydrocarbons and reaffirm the primacy of provincial resource ownership. That argument, however, came down to sharing economic rent between Alberta and the rest of the country, not whether those resources should be produced at all.

Even if the worst scenario unfolds — no additional pipelines, Bill C-69 enacted, and extreme, disproportionate national carbon policy — separation is not a practical option for Alberta, even though the threat of separation may have utility in dealing with the federal government, as it has proven over time to be useful for Quebec. The economic integration of Alberta with the rest of Canada cannot reasonably be undone. And it is impossible to know if Albertans would be prepared to seek closer economic and political integration with the United States in lieu of Canada. Would a Democratic administration ever bargain with an Alberta aspiring to leave Canada and to become the fifty-first state in the Union? Would it offer Alberta any better terms for its hydrocarbons than the current Trudeau government? In short, no.

Ironically, Alberta restored conservatives to lead its provincial government in April 2019, likely making it more difficult for the Trudeau government to rationalize reapproval of TMX. Such an Alberta government will deconstruct much of Notley's climate policy, while insisting, however legitimately, on market access regardless.

Of course, it remains unclear whether the Trudeau government can see reapproving TMX as "the right thing" at all, even if the project becomes the last market access alternative for Alberta. Trudeau may emulate Obama's 2015 KXL rejection, arguing that too much has changed since November 2016, that a reapproval would prove too harmful to Canada's climate credibility and its need to progress reconciliation. Easier to alienate four million relatively affluent Albertans, daring them to separate, knowing that most can't bring themselves to countenance actual separation.

Is the Trudeau government prepared to sacrifice the Alberta hydrocarbon economy? A bright line decision on reapproving TMX becomes the defining answer.

Delusions abound. Canada sits at the edge.

Epilogue

ON APRIL 16, 2019, Rachel Notley was defeated in her attempt to be re-elected premier of Alberta, losing by a margin of almost forty seats in an eighty-seven-seat legislature to the United Conservative Party led by Jason Kenney, which won over 50 percent of the popular vote in an election with a turnout of over 70 percent of the electorate.

Kenney, on the night of his election victory, reaffirmed his intention to deconstruct the major elements of the Notley climate plan established in late 2015, most notably its carbon tax and the oil sands emissions cap.

As of the end of April 2019, none of the remaining major pipeline projects — KXL, TMX, and LNG Canada's Coastal Gas Link — was yet under construction.

A week before the Alberta election, the federal government led by Justin Trudeau began imposing the carbon pricing backstop on those provinces that had not complied with the federal mandate as set out in the Pan-Canadian Framework. Several provinces have launched litigation against the federal government on account of this action.

Days after the Alberta election, the federal government announced a further delay in any reapproval of TMX until the middle of June 2019. On June 18, 2019, the Trudeau government reapproved TMX, inclusive of some accommodations arising from the additional First Nations consultation as mandated by the FCA. The government expressed its expectation that construction is to commence before year end. Days before, it had rejected all the material amendments to Bill C-69 that had been championed by the Canadian hydrocarbon industry.

Acknowledgements

THIS BOOK OWES MUCH to the staff at Dundurn Press, especially Dominic Farrell and Elena Radic, as well as freelance editor Cy Strom. Thank you to the network of colleagues, friends, and family who helped evolve my thinking on the visceral issues explored within this book. Jen Gerson provided especially astute insights that helped me clarify my arguments. Special thanks to Naomi Lewis for her many contributions to the realization of *Breakdown*. Thank you to Deborah Yedlin for generously providing the foreword. And as always, I am grateful for the vital support of my wife, Maureen.

Notes

INTRODUCTION

1. United States Department of State, *Final Supplemental Environmental Impact Statement for the Keystone XL Project,* U.S. Department of State (January 2014), accessed January 10, 2019, keystonepipeline -xl.state.gov/finalseis/.
2. Rebecca Joseph, "Pipeline Support Is Strong in Canada, but Provincial 'Divisions' Exist: Poll," *Global News,* January 16, 2019, globalnews.ca/news/4853116/canada-pipeline-crisis-poll/.

CHAPTER 1   SQUARING THE CIRCLE

1. "Canada," Climate Action Tracker, accessed January 12, 2019, climateactiontracker.org/countries/canada/.
2. "'Impossible' for Canada to Reach Kyoto Targets: Ambrose," *CBC News,* April 7, 2006, cbc.ca/news/canada/impossible-for-canada -to-reach-kyoto-targets-ambrose-1.583826.
3. "Turning the Corner Plan," Wikipedia, accessed January 19, 2019, en.wikipedia.org/wiki/Turning_the_Corner_Plan.

4. The cap-and-trade system offers an alternative to carbon pricing via a direct carbon tax. It specifies the quantity of emissions that may be emitted, and emitters bid for the right to emit within that cap, thereby creating a price. However, cap-and-trade structures are often complicated by specifics, such as how many sectors are covered, which emitters receive allowance to emit, and the allowance of alternative compliance mechanisms such as buying foreign offsets.

5. Matthew Bramley, "Far From Turning the Corner," Pembina Institute, June 20, 2008, pembina.org/op-ed/1661.

6. "Alberta SGER," Ecosystem Services, accessed January 13, 2019, eraecosystems.com/markets/alberta/.

7. "British Columbia Carbon Tax," Wikipedia, accessed January 13, 2019, en.wikipedia.org/wiki/British_Columbia_carbon_tax.

8. "Quebec to Collect Nation's 1st Carbon Tax," *CBC News,* June 7, 2007, cbc.ca/news/canada/montreal/quebec-to-collect-nation-s-1st-carbon-tax-1.684888.

9. Ontario, Ministry of Energy, Northern Development and Mines, "The End of Coal," Ontario.ca, accessed January 13, 2019, ontario.ca/page/end-coal.

10. Incremental emissions are emissions attributable to the production of oil sands that would not otherwise have existed, taking into account that the heavy oil demand would have been met by some other global heavy oil producer.

11. Les Whittington, "Dion's Carbon Tax Plan Was a Vote Loser, Ignatieff Says," *The Star* (Toronto), February 28, 2009, thestar.com/news/canada/2009/02/28/dions_carbon_tax_plan_was_a_vote_loser_ignatieff_says.html.

12. Northern Gateway was a new pipeline, planned to run due west from Edmonton and Kitimat and able to transport 800,000 barrels per day. The Trans Mountain expansion, TMX, was planned to utilize the existing pipeline route between Edmonton and Burnaby; its capacity was to be slightly smaller than that of the Northern Gateway pipeline. KXL was a direct pipeline connection between central Alberta and the U.S. Gulf Coast, traversing states including Montana, South Dakota, and Nebraska, on to the coast, with a scale on the order

of 800,000 to 1 billion barrels per day. Energy East's planned route went from central Alberta to Saint John, New Brunswick, utilizing the conversion of an existing but underutilized gas pipeline running between Alberta and Ontario, with a scale comparable to KXL.

13. Justin Trudeau. "Liberal Party of Canada Leader Justin Trudeau's Speech to the Calgary Petroleum Club," Liberal, October 30, 2013, liberal.ca/liberal-party-canada-leader-justin-trudeaus-speech-calgary -petroleum-club/.

14. WWF-Canada, "Why Doesn't WWF Propose a Different Route for the Northern Gateway Pipeline?" YouTube, May 31, 2012, youtube.com/watch?v=lWXRK4ffEH4.

15. "'Pipelines May Be Straight, but the Stories Behind Them Have Many Twists': How Kinder Morgan Was Approved," *National Post*, January 6, 2017, nationalpost.com/news/canada/pipelines-may-be-straight-but-the-stories-behind-them-have-many-twists-the-inside-story-of-kinder-morgans-approval.

16. Andrei Romaniuk and Hamid Rahmanifard, *Canadian Crude Oil and Natural Gas Production, Supply Costs, Economic Impacts and Emissions Outlook (2018–2038),* Study No. 173, July 2018, Canadian Energy Research Institute, ceri.ca/files/publications/316.

17. Marc Lee, "LNG Is Incompatible with BC's Climate Obligations," *Policynote*, July 11, 2018, policynote.ca/lng-is-incompatible-with-bcs-climate-obligations/.

18. Justin Trudeau, Prime Minister of Canada (official website), "Canada's National Statement at COP21," November 30, 2015, pm.gc.ca/eng/news/2015/11/30/canadas-national-statement-cop21.

19. "Alberta's NDP: Leadership for What Matters: Election Platform 2015,"AlbertaNDP.ca, accessed January 13, 2019, d3n8a8pro7vhmx.cloudfront.net/themes/5532a70ae-bad640927000001/attachments/original/1429634829/Alberta_NDP_Platform_2015.pdf?1429634829.

20. "Topp Releases Plan to Put the Environment at the Heart of the Economy," Brian Topp.ca, February 16, 2012, web.archive.org/web/20130407191759/http:/briantopp.ca/issues/topp-releases -plan-put-environment-heart-economy.

21. Government of Alberta, "Climate Leadership Plan Speech," Alberta.ca, November 22, 2015, alberta.ca/release.cfm?xID=38886 E9269850-A787-1C1E-A5C90ACF52A4DAE4; Andrew Leach et al., *Climate Leadership Report to Minister,* Alberta.ca, November 20, 2015, alberta.ca/documents/climate/climate-leadership-report-to-minister.pdf.
22. "'Pipelines May Be Straight,'" *National Post.*

CHAPTER 2 2016: INCOHERENCE AND CONTRADICTIONS

1. Darcy Henton, "Premiers Take 'Major Step Forward' on Climate Change: Endorse Urgent Approval of Pipelines, Says Notley," *Calgary Herald*, March 3, 2016, calgaryherald.com/news/politics/premiers-take-major-step-forward-on-climate-change-endorse-urgent-approval-of-pipelines-says-notley.
2. The Christy Clark government had set out five conditions for its support of oil pipeline infrastructure in British Columbia: (1) successful completion of the environmental assessment process; (2) world-leading marine oil-spill response systems in place; (3) world-leading mitigations and remediations relating to land-based oil spills; (4) legal requirements regarding Indigenous and treaty rights to be addressed; and (5) British Columbia to receive a fair share of the fiscal and economic benefits from the project.
3. National Energy Board, *National Energy Board Report: Trans Mountain Expansion Project (May 2016),* Environment Canada, ceaa-acee.gc.ca/050/documents/p80061/114562E.pdf.
4. Kyle Bakx, "Federal Government Has 7 Months to Make Decision on Controversial Project," *CBC News*, May 19, 2016, cbc.ca/news/business/pipeline-transmountain-neb-recommendation-1.3589518.
5. Environment and Climate Change Canada, *Trans Mountain Pipeline ULC — Trans Mountain Expansion Project: Review of Related Upstream Greenhouse Gas Emissions Estimates*, Canada.ca, November 2016, ceaa.gc.ca/050/documents/p80061/116524E.pdf.

6. Shawn McCarthy, "Liberal Government Formally Ratifies Paris Climate Accord," *Globe and Mail*, October 5, 2016, https://www.theglobeandmail.com/news/politics/ottawa-formally-ratifies-paris-climate-accord/article32267242/.

7. *Pan-Canadian Framework on Clean Growth and Climate Change: Canada's Plan to Address Climate Change and Grow the Economy*, Canada.ca, accessed December 21, 2018, canada.ca/content/dam/themes/environment/documents/weather1/20170125-en.pdf.

8. Bill McKibben, "Stop Swooning over Justin Trudeau: The Man Is a Disaster for the Planet," *Guardian* (International Edition), April 17, 2017, theguardian.com/commentisfree/2017/apr/17/stop-swooning-justin-trudeau-man-disaster-planet; Bill McKibben, "Say Hello to Justin Trudeau, the World's Newest Oil Executive," *Guardian* (International Edition), May 30, 2018, theguardian.com/commentisfree/2018/may/29/justin-trudeau-world-newest-oil-executive-kinder-morgan.

CHAPTER 3 2017: REVIVALS AND LOST OPTIONS

1. "Justin Trudeau's Speech in Houston: Read a Full Transcript," *Maclean's*, March 10, 2017, macleans.ca/economy/justin-trudeaus-speech-in-houston-read-a-full-transcript/.

2. "BP Energy Outlook: 2018 Edition," BP, 2018, bp.com/content/dam/bp/en/corporate/pdf/energy-economics/energy-outlook/bp-energy-outlook-2018.pdf.

3. Progress Energy Canada Ltd., *Pacific Northwest LNG: Project Description,* Environment Canada, ceaa.gc.ca/050/documents/p80032/86105E.pdf.

4. Pacific NorthWest LNG Limited Partnership and Stantec Consulting Ltd., *PNW LNG Project Design Mitigation,* Environment Canada, October 6, 2014, ceaa-acee.gc.ca/050/documents/p80032/100202E.pdf.

5. Catherine McKenna, "Decision Statement Issued under Section 54 of the *Canadian Environmental Assessment Act, 2012* […] for the Pacific

NorthWest LNG Project," Environment Canada, September 27, 2016, ceaa-acee.gc.ca/050/documents/p80032/115669E.pdf.

6. National Energy Board, "Memorandum of Understanding Between Environment and Climate Change Canada and the National Energy Board for the Establishment of a Public Engagement Process for the Assessment of Upstream Greenhouse Gas Emissions Related to the Energy East Project (MOU)," Canada.ca, December 17, 2015, neb-one.gc.ca/bts/ctrg/mmrndm/2016nvrnmntclmtchngcnd-eng .html?=undefined&wbdisable=true.

7. Pete Evans, "TransCanada Pulls Plug on Energy East Pipeline," *CBC News,* October 5, 2017, cbc.ca/news/business/transcanada-energy-east-1.4338227.

8. Tracy Johnson, "Energy East's Cause of Death: Business, Politics or Climate?" *CBC News*, October 6, 2017, cbc.ca/news/business/energy-east-transcanada-analysis-1.4341170.

CHAPTER 4 BILL C-69: POISON PILL

1. Jane Taber, "PM Brands Canada an 'Energy Superpower,'" *Globe and Mail*, July 15, 2006, theglobeandmail.com/news/world/pm-brands-canada-an-energy-superpower/article1105875/.

2. "Investment," Alberta.ca, January 14, 2019, economicdashboard .alberta.ca/Investment.

3. RCMP-GRC, "Critical Infrastructure Intelligence Assessment: Criminal Threats to the Canadian Petroleum Industry," State Watch, January 24, 2014, statewatch.org/news/2015/feb/can-2014-01-24-rcmp-anti-petroleum-activists-report.pdf.

4. Joe Oliver, "An Open Letter from Natural Resources Minister Joe Oliver," *Globe and Mail*, January 9, 2012, theglobeandmail.com/news/politics/an-open-letter-from-natural-resources-minister-joe-oliver/article4085663/.

5. Gerald Butts, "Deciding the Future of a Canadian Ecological Treasure," *WWF-Canada Blog: Climate*, January 11, 2012, blog.wwf.ca/blog/2012/01/11/deciding-the-future-of-a-canadian-ecological-

treasure/; Larry Lintz, "Elizabeth May's Cri de Coeur to Joe Oliver on Gateway," *Vancouver Sun*, January 11, 2012, vancouversun.com/news/staff-blogs/elizabeth-mays-cri-de-coeur-to-joe-oliver-on-gateway.

6. "Bill C-38," Parliament of Canada, April 26, 2012, parl.ca/DocumentViewer/en/41-1/bill/C-38/first-reading.

7. "Legal Backgrounder: The National Energy Board Act (1985)," Ecojustice, September, 2012, ecojustice.ca/wp-content/uploads/2015/03/SEPT-2012_FINAL_NEBA-backgrounder.pdf.

8. Butts, "Deciding the Future"; Gerald Butts, "Black Out Speak Out a Success, Thanks to YOU," *WWF-Canada Blog Community*, June 5, 2012, blog.wwf.ca/blog/2012/06/05/black-out-speak-out-a-success-thanks-to-you/.

9. Justin Trudeau, "Minister of Natural Resources Mandate Letter," Office of the Prime Minister, November 12, 2015, pm.gc.ca/eng/minister-natural-resources-mandate-letter.

10. Justin Trudeau, "Minister of Environment and Climate Change Mandate Letter," Office of the Prime Minister, November 12, 2015, pm.gc.ca/eng/minister-environment-and-climate-change-mandate-letter.

11. *Expert Panel Report: Building Common Ground: A New Vision for Impact Assessment in Canada*, Canada.ca, last modified June 28, 2017, canada.ca/en/services/environment/conservation/ assessments/environmental-reviews/environmental-assessment-processes/building-common-ground.html; *Forward, Together: Enabling Canada's Clean, Safe, and Secure Energy Future*, Natural Resources Canada, last modified December 21, 2017, nrcan.gc.ca/19667.

12. "Highlights from the National Energy Board Modernization Report," Dentons, May 23, 2017, dentons.com/en/insights/alerts/2017/may/23/highlights-from-the-national-energy-board-modernization-report.

13. "Bill C-69," Parliament of Canada, June 20, 2018, parl.ca/DocumentViewer/en/42-1/bill/C-69/third-reading; John Paul Tasker, "Ottawa to Scrap National Energy Board, Overhaul Environmental Assessment Process for Major Projects," *CBC News*, February 8, 2018, cbc.ca/news/politics/liberal-environmental-assessment-changes-1.4525666.

14. Canadian Press, "Alberta Environment Minister Says Federal Energy Bill C-69 Inadequate in Current Form," *Global News*, October 24, 2018, globalnews.ca/news/4592026/alberta-energy-projects-bill-C-69/; Shawn McCarthy, "Notley Demands Changes to Ottawa's Environmental Assessment Legislation," *Globe and Mail*, September 25, 2018, theglobeandmail.com/business/article-notley-demands-changes-to-ottawas-environmental-assessment/.

15. "CAPP Calls on Government to Pause on Bill C-69," *Context*, October 15, 2018, context.capp.ca/articles/2018/feature_capp-calls-on-government-to-pause-on-bill-c-69.

CHAPTER 5 MARCHING WITH YOUR FEET: TMX BUNGLED

1. "Trans Mountain Updates Customer Commitments for Proposed Expansion Project," Kinder Morgan Media & Investor Center, January 10, 2013, ir.kindermorgan.com/press-release/all/trans-mountain-updates-customer-commitments-proposed-expansion-project; "Trans Mountain Timeline: A Look at Key Dates in the Pipeline's History," *BNN Bloomberg*, May 29, 2018, bnnbloomberg.ca/trans-mountain-timeline-key-dates-in-the-history-of-the-pipeline-1.1051106.

2. Environment and Climate Change Canada, *Trans Mountain ULC — Trans Mountain Expansion Project*.

3. Kim Baird, Tony Penikett, and Dr. Annette Trimbee, *Report from the Ministerial Panel for the Trans Mountain Expansion Project (November 1, 2016)*, Natural Resources Canada, November 1, 2016, nrcan.gc.ca/sites/www.nrcan.gc.ca/files/files/pdf/16-011_TMX%20Full%20Report-en_nov2-11-30am.pdf.

4. Justine Hunter, Shawn McCarthy, and Jeff Lewis, "B.C. Takes Pipeline Fight to Court, Asking for Power to Restrict Oil Shipments," *Globe and Mail*, April 26, 2018, theglobeandmail.com/canada/british-columbia/article-bc-seeks-jurisdiction-over-oil-shipments-with-court-reference/; National Energy Board, "NEB Issues Ruling

on Process for Future Permitting Matters, and Reasons for Decision on Trans Mountain Expansion Project Constitutional Question," Canada.ca, January 18, 2018, neb-one.gc.ca/bts/nws/nr/2018/nr04-eng.html?=undefined&wbdisable=true; Laura Kane, "B.C. Government to Join First Nations, Municipalities in Trans Mountain Pipeline Legal Action," *The Star* (Toronto), August 10, 2017, thestar.com/business/2017/08/10/bc-government-looks-to-join-first-nations-municipalities-in-trans-mountain-pipeline-legal-action.html; Ian Bailey, "B.C. First Nations Unite in Fight Against Trans Mountain Pipeline," *Globe and Mail*, January 17, 2017, theglobeandmail.com/news/british-columbia/bc-first-nations-unite-in-fight-against-trans-mountain-pipeline/article33653315/.

5. "Schedule 14A," United States Securities and Exchange Commission, accessed January 14, 2019, sec.gov/Archives/edgar/data/1506307/000104746918002313/a2234931zdef14a.htm; Jesse Snyder and Geoffrey Morgan, "Ottawa Offers Financial Backstop for Trans Mountain Pipeline amid Continued Pushback in B.C.," *Financial Post*, May 16, 2018, business.financialpost.com/commodities/energy/ottawa-offers-financial-backstop-for-trans-mountain-pipeline-amid-continued-pushback-in-b-c.

6. The long-term ownership of TMX, once constructed and operating, remains an open question. The federal government is unlikely to want to be a long-term owner, but will prefer to recover its investment and apply those funds to other government priorities. Whether ownership over the long run will be dictated solely by financial considerations, or whether some viable mechanism evolves to create a share of First Nations ownership in TMX, remains to be resolved.

CHAPTER 6   LATE 2018: BLOWS ON A BRUISE

1. Karen Graham, "Federal Judge Blocks Keystone XL Pipeline," *Digital Journal*, November 9, 2018, digitaljournal.com/news/politics/federal-judge-blocks-keystone-xl-pipeline/article/536481#.ixzz5WxldQpnT; United States Department of State,

Final Supplemental Environmental Impact Statement for the Keystone XL Project.

2. Shawn McCarthy and Justin Giovannetti, "Call for Crude Production Quotas Splits Oil Patch," *Globe and Mail*, November 15, 2018, theglobeandmail.com/business/article-call-for-crude-production-quotas-splits-oil-patch/.

3. Robert Tuttle, "Heavy Canadian Crude Falls to Record Low amid Production Cuts," *Bloomberg*, November 15, 2018, bloomberg.com/news/articles/2018-11-15/heavy-canadian-crude-falls-to-record-low-amid-production-cuts.

4. Dan Healing, "Economic Cost of Canadian Oil Price Discounts Counted in Billions of Dollars," *CBC News*, November 11, 2018, cbc.ca/news/canada/calgary/canadian-oil-price-discounts-impact-1.4901147.

5. "The Tar Sands Campaign," CorpEthics, accessed December 28, 2018, corpethics.org/the-tar-sands-campaign/.

6. U.S. Global Change Research Program, *Fourth National Climate Assessment: Volume II: Impacts Risks, and Adaptation in the United States*, 2018, nca2018.globalchange.gov/.

7. UN Environment, "Emissions Gap Report 2018," United Nations Environment Programme, November 27, 2018, unenvironment.org/resources/emissions-gap-report-2018.

8. Josh Wingrove and Kevin Orland, "Canada Offers $1.1 Billion in Loans for Oil-Sector Liquidity," *Bloomberg*, December 18, 2018, bloomberg.com/news/articles/2018-12-18/canada-said-to-offer-1-1-billion-in-loan-support-for-oil-sector; Josh Wingrove, "Oil Industry Loans from Feds Are Not What Alberta Asked For: Notley," *BNN Bloomberg*, December 18, 2018, bnnbloomberg.ca/canada-to-offer-1-1-billion-in-loan-support-for-oil-sector-1.1185135.

CHAPTER 7   FINDING A WAY

1. Natural Resources Canada, *Energy and the Economy,* Canada.ca, accessed January 15, 2019, nrcan.gc.ca/energy/facts/energy-economy/20062.

2. Natural Resources Canada, *Energy Fact Book 2016–2017*, Canada. ca, nrcan.gc.ca/sites/nrcan.gc.ca/files/energy/pdf/EnergyFact-Book_2016_17_En.pdf.

3. Natural Resources Canada, *Energy and the Economy.*

CHAPTER 8   A RATIONAL APPROVAL PROCESS

1. United States Department of State, *Final Supplemental Environmental Impact Statement for the Keystone XL Project;* Environment and Climate Change Canada, *Trans Mountain Pipeline ULC.*

2. "Trudeau Talks About Bill C-69 to Alberta's Chamber of Commerce," *Global News*, November 22, 2018, globalnews.ca/video /4690204/trudeau-talks-about-bill-c-69-to-albertas-chamber-of-commerce.

CHAPTER 9   CLIMATE POLICY FOR CANADA — TO UNIFY OR TO POLARIZE?

1. Environment and Climate Change Canada, *Canadian Environmental Sustainability Indicators: Greenhouse Gas Emissions,* Canada. ca, accessed December 28, 2018, ec.gc.ca/indicateurs-indicators/ default.asp?lang=En&n=FBF8455E-1.

2. Environment and Climate Change Canada, *Canadian Environmental Sustainability Indicators: Greenhouse Gas Emissions,* Canada.ca, accessed December 28, 2018, canada.ca/en/environment -climate-change/services/environmental-indicators/greenhouse -gas-emissions.html.

3. Dan Healing, "Approving LNG Canada Project Could Tap into Glut of Alberta Natural Gas," *Global News*, September 28, globalnews.ca/news/4498482/approving-lng-canada-alberta-natural-gas/; National Energy Board, *Marketable Natural Gas Production in Canada,* Canada.ca, November 22, 2018, neb-one.gc.ca/nrg/sttstc/ ntrlgs/stt/mrktblntrlgsprdctn-eng.html.

4. "The CAT Thermometer," Climate Action Tracker, accessed December 28, 2018, climateactiontracker.org/global/cat-thermometer/.

5. Michael Bastach, "Limiting Global Warming Could Cost $122 Trillion: That's 'Not Feasible,' Says One Economist," *Daily Caller*, November 9, 2018, dailycaller.com/2018/10/09/limiting-global -warming-cost/.

6. Katharine Ricke, "Country-Level Social Cost of Carbon," *Nature Climate Change* 8 (2018), 895-900, nature.com/articles/ s41558-018-0282-y.

7. Trottier Energy Futures Project Partners, *Canada's Challenge and Opportunity: Transformations for Major Reductions in GHG Emissions,* David Suzuki Foundation, April 2016, davidsuzuki.org/science -learning-centre-article/report-canadas-challenge-opportunity -transformations-major-reductions-ghg-emissions/.

8. Government of Canada, "Pathway to Meeting Canada's 2030 Tar-get," Canada.ca, accessed January 16, 2019, canada.ca/en/services/ environment/weather/climatechange/pan-canadian-framework/ pathway-canada-target.html.

9. "USA," Climate Action Tracker, 2018, climateactiontracker.org/ countries/usa/, accessed December 22, 2018.

10. Environment and Climate Change Canada, *Carbon Dioxide Emissions from a Consumption Perspective,* Canada.ca, accessed December 28, 2018, ec.gc.ca/indicateurs-indicators/default.asp?lang=en&n=F.

11. Michael Tutton, "'I'm No Quitter' on Climate Change Issues, McKenna Says at G7 Ministers Meeting," *Financial Post*, September 19, 2018, business.financialpost.com/pmn/business-pmn/young-people-need-us-to-act-on-climate-change-mckenna-tells-g7-ministers.

12. Chris Varcoe, "Varcoe: Canadians Believe a Pipeline Crisis Has Arrived and Say Ottawa Needs to Do More," *Calgary Herald*, January 16, 2019, calgaryherald.com/opinion/columnists/varcoe-canadians-believe-a-pipeline-crisis-has-arrived-and-say-ottawa-needs-to-do-more-poll; Rebecca Joseph, "Majority of Canadians Support Trans Mountain Pipeline Expansion: Ipsos Poll," *Global News*, May 2, 2018, globalnews.ca/news/4180482/majority-of-canadians-support-trans-mountain-pipeline-expansion-ipsos-poll/; Matto

Mildenberger et al., "The Distribution of Climate Change Public Opinion in Canada," *PLoS One* 11, no. 8 (August 3, 2016), dx.doi.org/10.1371%2Fjournal.pone.0159774.

13. David Suzuki and Ian Hanington, "Audit Exposes Canadian Climate Failures," David Suzuki Foundation, April 5, 2018, davidsuzuki.org/story/audit-exposes-canadian-climate-failures/.

CHAPTER 10 AN INCONVENIENT REALITY

1. "Section 35 of the Constitution Act, 1982," Wikipedia, accessed December 28, 2018, en.wikipedia.org/wiki/Section_35_of_the_Constitution_Act,_1982.
2. "*Tsilhqot'in Nation v. British Columbia*," *Judgments of the Supreme Court of Canada*, June 26, 2014, scc-csc.lexum.com/scc-csc/scc-csc/en/item/14246/index.do?site_preference=normal.

CHAPTER 11 BREAKDOWN

1. "Nearly 6 in 10 Canadians Polled Call Lack of New Pipeline Capacity a 'Crisis,'" *CBC News,* January 16, 2019, cbc.ca/news/canada/british-columbia/pipeline-capacity-poll-1.4979805.

Further Reading

Canada's EcoFiscal Commission, *The Way Forward: A Practical Approach to Reducing Canada's Greenhouse Gas Emissions*, 2015, https://ecofiscal. ca/reports/wayforward/.

Climate Tracker, "Some progress since Paris, but not enough, as governments amble towards 3°C of warming," December 2018, https:// climateactiontracker.org/publications/warming-projections-global-update-dec-2018/.

Climate Tracker, *Transformation Points — Achieving the Speed and Scale Required for Full Decarbonisation*, April 2019, https:// climateactiontracker.org/publications/transformation-points/.

Environment and Climate Change Canada, *Canadian Environmental Sustainability Indicators: Greenhouse Gas Emissions*, April 2019, https://www.canada.ca/content/dam/eccc/documents/pdf/ cesindicators/ghg-emissions/2019/national-GHG-emissions-en.pdf.

ExxonMobil, *2018 Outlook for Energy: A View to 2040*, https://corporate. exxonmobil.com/en/Energy-and-environment/Energy-resources/ Outlook-for-Energy/2018-Outlook-for-Energy-A-View-to-2040.

Federal Court of Appeal, *Tsleil-Waututh Nation v. Canada (Attorney General)*, August 2018, https://decisions.fca-caf.gc.ca/fca-caf/ decisions/en/item/343511/index.do#_Remedy.

Government of Canada, *PanCanadian Framework on Clean Growth and Climate Change*, 2017, https://www.canada.ca/content/dam/themes/environment/documents/weather1/20170125-en.pdf.

Government of Canada, *PanCanadian Framework on Clean Growth and Climate Change: Second Annual Synthesis Report on the Status for Implementation — December 2018*, http://publications.gc.ca/collections/collection_2018/eccc/En1-77-2018-eng.pdf.

Intergovernmental Panel on Climate Change, *2014 Synthesis Report: Summary for Policymakers, International Panel on Climate Change*, https://archive.ipcc.ch/pdf/assessment-report/ar5/syr/AR5_SYR_FINAL_SPM.pdf.

Intergovernmental Panel on Climate Change, *Special Report: Global Warming of 1.5ºC, Summary for Policymakers*, 2018, https://www.ipcc.ch/sr15/chapter/summary-for-policy-makers/.

International Energy Agency, *World Energy Outlook 2018*, https://webstore.iea.org/download/summary/190?fileName=English-WEO-2018-ES.pdf

Leach, Andrew, et al. *Climate Leadership: Report to Minister, Government of Alberta, Government of Alberta*, 2015, https://www.alberta.ca/documents/climate/climate-leadership-report-to-minister.pdf.

National Energy Board of Canada, *National Energy Board — NEB Report — OH-001-2014 (A77045)* [TransMountain Expansion Project], May 2016, https://apps.neb-one.gc.ca/REGDOCS/Item/Filing/A77045.

Image Credits

Index

Book Credits

Acquiring Editor: Dominic Farrell
Project Editor: Elena Radic
Editorial Assistant: Melissa Kawaguchi
Copy Editor: Cy Strom

Designer: Laura Boyle
Cover Designer: Sophie Paas-Lang

Publicist: Saba Eitizaz